A Name
for
Ourselves

feelings about
authentic identity
love
intuitive politics
us

A NAME
FOR
OURSELVES

BY PAUL POTTER

foreword by Leni Wildflower

Little, Brown and Company
Boston · Toronto

306
P86n

To Kenneth and Eve Potter
my father and mother

Contents

Acknowledgments   ix

Foreword   xiii

1   About the Book   3

Part 1 : Experience   13

2   The Meaninglessness of Words   15

3   The Meaninglessness of Experience   26

4   Love   46

5   Images of Love   53

6   Love and Sex   73

Contents

Part 2 : Class and Separatism 87

7 Separatism 89
8 We Are Not Middle-Class 100
9 We Are Not Working-Class 121

Part 3 : Ideological Projects 129

10 Ideology — Under *R* for Revolution 131
11 The Economic Research and Action Project 136
12 Youth Culture 154
13 Why I Like Women's Liberation 169

Part 4 : Images of the Future 177

14 Toward a Revolutionary Separatist Church and the Great Council of Revolutionary Separatist Movements 179
15 The Pressure for Definition 192
16 Images of the Future 197

Part 5 : Postscript 209

Acknowledgments

When I think about who I might acknowledge for help in writing this book, my mind begins to wander far back into my childhood to people I have not seen or heard from for many years — early childhood friends, a student teacher in a nursery school who I only remember as Miss Grapejuice, a man I met in a store once, the people I grew up with in Champaign and Mahomet and Charlotte, relatives, friends from college, friends from politics, from Philadelphia, Ann Arbor, Atlanta, Cleveland, Boston, all the people in my life now, people who are no longer alive.

I think of so many people over such a span of time and

places because in fact it is that collective that has made my life real — the collective of all the people who were real and in some sense positive in my life — even though I drifted so easily away from so many, left a few in anger, parted from so many more in frustration and guilt and despair. I think of so many people, and it is tempting to call each of you by name here, to use the knowledge that this book will find its way into many of your hands as a vehicle for touching fragments of my past and holding parts of the present. But it is too hard. The mere contemplation of it sends my mind spiraling back into thoughts about how we were together, what we did, how we hurt and helped, how we looked at each other. But it seems strangely immoral to make that list. It is not the way my life works. It is not what my mind wants to do. But if I cannot bring myself to reach back and name you, I can acknowledge you and thank you and say that I see most of you more clearly now than when we were last together, find that as I have grown, my memory of more and more relationships has deepened, and I have seen what my thinness of spirit clouded at the time. It is the reality that came from so many people that made me believe I could write a book out of my own (our) experience. If you don't like it, I will allow you to take some of the credit for it, because you also hid from me. That is not a criticism; just a statement of the obvious fact that this book can be no more than what we were to each other.

I do want to mention my foundation, however. This book was written off and on over a period of three years, most of the time without the aid of any grant or advance. I was able to work on it because people lent me their homes, money in some cases, and even the typewriter the book was written on. Some of those people are Jim Morey, Bob Rosenthal, Chris Rosenthal, Penny Patch, Chris Williams, Annie Williams, Merilee Todd Russell, Bea Zeiger, Irv Zeiger, Joyce Unger, Richard Unger, Louis Kampf, Norman Potter.

Finally, there are three people who were most closely connected to the writing of the book itself. Joan Culver helped to push me out the door of our Cambridge crisis and into New Hampshire and the beginning of the book. I needed the help. Dickie Magidoff not only talked to me about much of what I was trying to think through with the book and liked it when I was afraid nobody would, but also, more than any other person, helped me to feel that it was legitimate for me to concentrate on me.

Leni Wildflower brought so many changes to me and the book that I have simply lost track. There is no separating her "contributions" from mine. The book began to be written at about the time my relationship with Leni began, and more and more, over time, it took root in the reality of that relationship. Our deepest conflicts led to the recognition of what to me feel like some of the most important parts of the book. Our most deeply shared feelings created an environment to be alive in, a place where we could see and think, a way to explore much more than I had ever explored before.

Foreword

I will not write an introduction to this book. Writing an introduction feels to me like being an ornament, an accessory for Paul's book. I will not be an ornament. I will not "usher in" the book. Will not lubricate it, make it easy. The book will either stand or fall on its own anyway.

But I do want to say something right here in the front of this book. If I take Paul's book seriously — believe that it is *most important* to understand and talk about and seek validation for my own experience — then it makes sense that I should write here in this book what I am feeling. How much anger I feel when I simply feel my own experience. How much love.

But when I write that, no one believes it is "right" for the book. Somehow it establishes the "wrong tone." It's too embarrassing, even for my friends who are in some way moved by it. It seems to "go off on its own tack." Of course. That is the point.

My *experience* is different from Paul's. My *tone* is different from Paul's. I will not establish my validity through his words or his voice. Paul's tone sounds to me like a male luxury I never had. Once I desperately wanted that tone. Now I don't. Paul's tone is smooth, analytical, sensitive, yet too removed from the very emotions he talks about. He is persuasive and at ease with words. You like him because he uses life-examples which we all can identify with. And he is even willing to identify with *you* (which can in fact be a clever way to avoid confronting you). My voice is not at home with these qualities in Paul's writing. My tone *is* abrasive.

My *experience* over the last several years has been one of steadily getting closer to the bare living bone of my feelings. And if the book says anything, it says my experience is important for you to hear about. It says if you can hear what I am saying you will know something about yourself — and that if you can't you will deny something in you. And if you feel my feelings are out of place here, now, or when you have read the book, then I believe you have misunderstood what this book is trying to be about.

What is most real in my life is my anger and pain at men — all men. Starting with my father, including Paul, and right down to eight-year-old Michael. But mostly my anger and hurt and humiliation is at my generation, "my people." That is, young men, hip men, revolutionary men. And it is there because it is you men who pose as the bearers of the new liberation, of new life-styles for us all. You claim to have rejected the old order and tell me you are creating a new one — through flowers or bombs or baking bread. But that is a myth, a lie, because the images (freaks or revolutionaries) may be new but you still need me (a woman and all women) to keep you propped up. New images, but at rock bottom, the same old male ego and the same fanatic devotion to keeping women "womanly."

Here they come. Those strutting roosters, those pathetic male chauvinists, egocentric, pompous and ridiculous bastards. Here come the freaks in those tight bell-bottoms, tie-dyed T-shirt which their "old lady" (would you believe it?) made for them. Cowboy boots, swagger walk, wide leather belt with the great big brass buckle. And don't forget the hair, the oh so long hair. But in the end the still oh so masculine hair. (I have never seen a hip man I couldn't identify from the back.) And they parade in my world and in my eyes they have all the grooviness and cooled-out posture of those beer-drinking, madras-dressed, women-fucking frat rats I saw in college. (At least frat rats gave their women the dignity of openly treating them like a piece of property — which is more honest than the love freaks who spend most of their time adamantly denying that they are anything but gentle, cooled-out people.) Yes, gentle and cooled out, having given up the competitive American struggle in the great wide world. Just living, making mellow vibes, teaching their women to be cool, storing up contempt for the straight world or anybody who is "up tight" or any situation that is "too heavy." Exhausting themselves staying groovy.

Hip men aren't the only men who parade through my world. There are those long-haired, chest-pounding, rhetoric-slinging revolutionaries. All of them have "confessed" their chauvinism, over and over again. Some are going to "purge" themselves of their oppressive natures; some are going to "struggle" against it. All of them give "the problem" a few paragraphs in their analysis. And they are going to build a new society for us all — if we women could just forget our petty bourgeois grievances (women talking about women problems) and *do something*. Like get behind the barricades to fight the capitalist pig empire. They know so well about my problem. Here they go, waving me around, Mao in one hand, and the other tying me and my oppression up in little red knots. Yes, here they go, fist in the air, feet stomping, shouting, "Smash male chauvinism. Smash male chauvinism." That has to be laughable!

Young men, hip men, revolutionary men, freaks everywhere, can't you see? I never expected anything from the frat rats. I once expected something from you. Male liberators, *you* are stepping on my neck. And the reality of that pain — the pain that never alters, that only for moments lets up — keeps me feeling mad so much of the time. The reality of that pain is the deepest reality of my life. It gives me a starkness that makes me demand straightness from *all* my friends, male and female. My most fundamental need is for real contact with the people around me — regardless of whether that is "negative" or "positive" contact.

I am trying desperately to peel away the layers of lies — trying to pull back the skin of society, school, family. The expectations which somewhere along the line got internalized. The desire to "be something," the pretty deep conviction that I am *nothing.* Losing my capacity to know what I am. Listening to others tell me what to look like or what a nice girl I once was or how I behave or how I ought to behave. And in the middle of my quest there are all these men laying their power-ego-identity trips on me.

The anger for men. My love for Paul. Winter afternoons in New Hampshire — long lazy endless time filled with talk. Making new ideas — new kinds of talk — different ways of thinking, my mind crackling alive with excitement. Paul and Leni. Leni and Paul. Struggling together, clinging together — across the country — New Hampshire, Cambridge, through the Chicago ordeal, out to Berkeley, now here in Felton. Learning how to fight. The commitment deepening. My anger for Paul growing with the love — romantic tentative touch love at first; then love deepening, feeling more easy, love feeling steady, love feeling lasting.

The building of a relationship. A space for validation which has freed enormous energy in me, my thoughts and feelings and activities: "Yes, Leni, that *is* real. The fears are real. I can see them and begin to feel with you. I see your pain and feel fury at a society which made you hate yourself and distrust your emotions. I fear your anger, but I feel the integrity of it. Your anger is connecting. Your anger is good for people. Your rage has hawk eyes."

But Paul and our relationship have also brought the pain and anger and humiliation up very close. Feeling dependent, afraid, resentful, unsure — feeling oppressed. Yet when I recognize and respond to Paul's chauvinism, to the oppressive qualities in a man I live with, it begins to make it possible for some real closeness to exist between us.

At the bottom of it all — all the anger, all the rage and the hunger for validation, all the love — at the bottom is still my sense of myself as an oppressed woman. An identity which is bankrupt, grim, raw — and bare. Bare because all other identities which once defined me have been peeled back. But I do have roots. As a woman I have come to find the deepest roots — the roots of an oppressed *human being*. They are more powerful than any force I have ever experienced. They have opened incredible love for other women. And the web that binds the roots and holds them firm is trust in the intuitive Leni. Believing in my anger, feeling fears and knowing they are justified, spitting out my rage with a freedom which sometimes literally sings out and makes my body soar. And I know at those moments the strength and beauty and love which lives inside me.

Out of all this a new Leni began to grow and rise up in anger and fear and love and clarity. And a relationship grew and stretched, reached out, and took us to new places. And *A Name for Ourselves* was written.

with love for my best friend,
Leni Wildflower
February 1971

A Name
for
Ourselves

1

About the Book

I have struggled for some time with the problem of what this book is about. The project was originally presented to me in connection with a course I was helping to teach at MIT on intellectuals and social change. Andre Schiffrin, editor of Pantheon Books, was working on a set of "anti-text" books that would explore radical or at least non-Establishment approaches to the social sciences. He talked to Louis Kampf and Noam Chomsky, the creators of the course, and asked them if they would do a book on intellectuals and social change — a sort of meta-anti-text that would demonstrate from a radical perspective how the American intellectual community had got itself into the business of being the prime apologist for the status quo and point presumably to the directions in which change could and was taking place. Kampf and Chomsky were into other things — teaching and writing of their own — plus spending tremendous amounts of time traveling and speaking, trying to put together a national anti-draft support group called Resist. I, on the other hand, was not. My latest political adventure, a Boston movement school called the Educational Cooperative, had collapsed in the fall, leaving me suspended and in doubt — looking for a thing to do, a place to attach myself in the crazy-quilt assortment of events called trying-to-build-a-movement-for-social-change-in-America. At the time, I had started working in a factory to keep my head straight, my hands busy, pay off some debts, and find out what working in a factory is like. (It is very hard.)

When Noam and Louis approached me and asked me if I would do the book, it seemed right. It would "force me to think," provide money to pay debts, and yet remain a limited project — something that would be done when it was done. Besides, working on the book would parallel the teaching I would be doing during the spring term at MIT. I did an outline of what I would write, talked to some people, including Schiffrin, and concluded that the ideas still seemed sound. The decision was made.

But for the umpteenth time in my life, I learned that things just ain't that simple. The decision began to feel like a straitjacket. What business did I have writing a book anyway? It certainly wasn't as if I was bursting with some news I wanted to get into print while I stuffed potatoes in a can in a factory. I was in the factory in the first place because in some sense I'd run out of the compulsion to go around talking to people. Furthermore, when I was frank, I admitted that I didn't put all that much stock in writing. It wasn't as if I'd picked up Marx or Mao or Jefferson or anyone else and had the world change in front of my eyes. If anything, it was the other way around. It was only when my world had begun to change that some writers I considered important began to come into focus, make sense, and help to articulate what I already felt.

The clincher was my students. They were bright, well read, wrote insightfully, and impressed me in many ways as being more advanced intellectually and politically than I was at their age. Furthermore, most of them had entered the class because of growing anxiety about the state of the world and a desire to keep their minds and their lives from becoming tools of the ugliness in it. There was less constraint in the classroom than I had ever experienced as an undergraduate — no exams, voluntary attendance in lectures and discussions, little pressure about grades. And yet, despite all this, the most essential feature of being a class remained intact — ideas were abstract and formal, things were approached academically. My students seemed to me to be very successful schizophrenics. Their lives, the good things and the bad things, the things that turned them on or made them die inside, were left at the door of the class or on the first page of an assigned book. When they entered my discussion section, they entered "the great world of ideas," somehow strained dry by definition of any vital potential to reflect on the rest of their existence. There were a billion words available to describe a million "interesting" things, and we used them all without ever once believing very much in the efficacy of the words or the reality of what they described — revolution, intellectuals, black people, war, school, education, change, work — all powerful words, but all dead. I wanted to strike all my students and myself mute for a week or a month. "You get no more words or maybe two or a dozen at the most and you can only use each of them once." (Quiet.)

All the time I was thinking these things I was supposed to be working on a book. Or maybe I should say, because I was supposed to be working on a book and didn't know why, I started looking at my class with new eyes. What would a book *do?* Where would it go? How would it penetrate the armor that had been hammered together, more or less successfully, by fourteen years of extraneous ideas? I began to understand that I could write a thorough, scholarly critique of the intellectual community that all my students would "understand" and find "challenging" and "relevant," and still wind up speaking to no one in the way I wanted to. I discovered, among other things, that I have very little interest in truth as such. If you could pile all the truth in the world together in one big (or perhaps little) heap but could do nothing with it, could communicate it to no one in a useful way, I'm afraid I would take no satisfaction from knowing that it existed or had been accumulated. But that is precisely what most people who write books convince themselves they are for — accumulating truth, adding another grain of wisdom to the warehouse of human knowledge. I would almost be willing to communicate a lie, if it could cut through, if it could rupture the vacuum that has grown up around our minds. If truth is just a heap, a stack of books and tables and calipers, functioning in a humanless, remote, autonomous sphere, then I want nothing to do with it. If my book was "correct" but unconnected to people, then I wanted to scrap the whole project.

When it was time to sign a contract with the publisher, the original idea of the book was crushed. Its formal structure seemed worthless. Most of the research I'd done in preparation seemed irrelevant. But the process of casting off my original conception had left me with some hard nuggets of interest. There were in fact some things I was looking for a way to say — problems that had been spinning around in my own head that I would like to have shared more with my students, had I only known how. There was a set of insights and observations and feelings that I wanted to get out that was both autobiographical and political. At first, it seemed curious that the two should be merged in my mind. But as I thought about it, I realized that it was precisely the separation of biography and politics into separate and remote categories that so upset me in my class. Although I wasn't very clear about what I wanted to say, not nearly as clear as I'd been about the original idea, not nearly clear enough to get a book contract or an advance, I was certain that the problem of biography and politics was the only one that was important enough to me to justify writing a book. It was, after all, what I wanted and had been unable to talk to my students about — how their lives connected to politics in a way that meant something. And it was also, if I could admit it, what I needed to talk to myself about. Because politics and my life were not getting on too well together. Even though I still felt deeply committed to the movement, I was unable to find a place for myself in it that seemed right. My life and my politics were altogether more separable then I wanted them to be.

So with this problem fairly close to the front of my mind, I stowed my original plan, and made my first attempt to clarify the new one. Actually, the very first thing I did was to write part of the chapter you are reading now, to get down on paper just where I was starting from and how I had gotten there. Now when I look back on that first attempt, I can sense how much my thinking has changed over the one and a half years that I have worked more or less sporadically on this writing. But basically, this book still turns out to be about making life connected to politics. And although I feel quite differently about both my life and my politics than I did when I started, I still feel the problem I started out with was the right problem. Indeed, I still feel it is the problem — because I have not solved it. What writing the book has done for me, and what I hope reading and thinking about it will do for you, is give me a framework of approaching the problem. My head is clearer even though many things are hardly resolved.

In America the essential difference between politics and biography is point of view. From one, history is seen as some-

thing that has happened to an individual — he calls it "his life."
From the other, history is seen as something that has happened
to someone else — like "the workers," or "black people," or
"the poor." And in fact, the way history is written in this
country, there is a tendency to lose track of people altogether.
History becomes a formal thing with no particular reference
to people — or even historical forces. We learn about checks
and balances, courts and Congress and of course elections.
Those are the things that happen in history that our political
theorists observe in order to make political theory. In government, things get "checked"; in court, "famous" decisions get
"made"; and of course, in elections, great men get elected.
Great men, in due time, write their biographies to explain
how *they* did it. And we, in our own time, though usually not
of our own free will, read both the political theory and the biography, and conclude quite correctly that none of it has anything to do with us.

If we identify with either, it must be with the biography,
since that is about a person, even if his enormity and sagacity
or the mere fact of his stature and elevation makes our own
lives seem the more pale and drab by comparison. Naturally,
no ordinary person has any business writing his biography,
since by definition his life is as tedious as the next. A couple
of crackpot anthropologists have taken an interest in the biography of "ordinary" people — but on close examination, their
folk turn out to be "exotic" or "ethnic," as far removed from
our lives in their own way as are the great men. We are left
with the possibility of more or less secretly identifying with
some great man, of mingling our own power fantasies with his,
of dreaming that someday we might be like him.

But of course there is a price for identifying with the great
man. The caricature of it is the megalomaniac in his padded
cell screaming orders to the insane. The more grotesque reality
is the Johnsons and the Kennedys and the Nixons, pushing their
fantasies to the top of the heap and threatening to annihilate

anything that gets in the way. And as always, the most mundane, most oppressive example, is our own burden of lugging all those big men around in our heads, only to hear them say what small and insignificant porters of their grandeur we are.

In the final analysis, it is not even a question of how "successful" we are in identifying with the biographies of the great, in imagining how our own biographies could be like theirs, or for that matter, whether we actually succeed in becoming LBJs or Caesars. The price we pay is the loss of respect for the other identity, the ordinary one, the only one that was uniquely our own, and the only one that despite its uniqueness could be shared with a lot of other people. The price we pay is *real* insignificance and isolation. By insignificance, I mean the destruction of an authentic, loving self and the creation of a self-hating creature driven by external images. By isolation, I mean being separated from our own, from men in search of their wholeness.

It is not at all clear that biography and politics are always such separate things. In revolutionary settings biography and politics merge in a way that is difficult for our minds to comprehend. Edgar Snow, in *Red Star Over China*, complained that it was very difficult for him to pry loose biographical information from the leaders of the revolution. They seemed almost unaware of their own "stories," reluctant and uncomfortable in talking about themselves. But at a moment's notice they could talk at great length and in vivid detail about the Long March or any other stage of the revolutionary struggle. Or again, people are almost invariably disappointed when they read Che's *Reminiscences*. With the exception of some correspondence that was included at the end, the book itself is a rather flat, colorless, sometimes technical description of what went on in the Sierra Maestra. One learns little of the great man himself. In fact, he seems plain, only ordinarily intelligent and ordinarily humorless, almost passionless, even a little puritanical, hardly worth all the fuss. What excites him is the same as might excite any soldier — being promoted for valor and experience, being entrusted with one of the few really good weapons the rebels had captured. Most everyone concludes that the great man's modesty cloaks his genius, or perhaps that he is just not a very good writer. No one is willing to venture the observation that perhaps Che, like the people he led, was a very ordinary man.

But that is not exactly the point either. The point is not whether Che was a particularly great man or not. It is rather that at certain times and places in history, the antagonism between biography and political thought subsides. You ask a man about himself and he tells you about his people. You ask a woman about her children and she speaks of all children. You ask a leader what he did to lead his people to freedom and he tells you about the life and trials of a guerrilla soldier.

We of course have been told that what this phenomenon represents is the merciless subjugation of the individual to the collective, a kind of depersonalization that goes on so the revolutionary despot can command fanatic loyalty from his followers. But I want to suggest something else. I want to begin this book by asking people to suspend judgment awhile, to try to open themselves to another possibility. The proposition itself is quite simple. It is that our sense of self is false; that our "identities" are based on an antagonism and competition with the people who should be "our folks" — that is, the people who are most like us. That our attempt to build a life story, an authentic biography, is essentially the process by which we isolate ourselves from our neighbors by putting them down and competing with them. And the corollary of this is that the blending of biography and politics for the revolutionary is the very thing that makes him a whole man, an authentic person. It is the recognition, conscious or not, that his life (his biography, his politics) is significant insofar as it represents a bond forged between himself and other people against the

great men who made history, politics and biography their
preserve.

By now you may be wondering about my repeated use of
the word "we," and since I will continue to use it frequently
in the rest of the book, some explanation of who I think "we"
are is in order. The fact is that I don't know. This book will
begin to serve its purpose if "we" can be helped by it to sort
ourselves out — if some of the people who read this book can
use it to see each other in a new light. We are the people who
today for the most part see each other as "them." If we could
learn to recognize one another, we would be very powerful.

One more note. This book is written in many voices. I am
quite certain that in the normal sense of style it is an atrocity.
There are fairly jarring breaks in the tone, phrasing and level
from one chapter to the next. But I cannot bring myself to
try to rewrite the book all in one voice. What made the book
worthwhile for me to work on was that it kept opening me up
to new ways of looking at things — kept changing my feelings and consequently the way I put words together, the kind
of voice I used. Somehow I cannot get excited about making
a consistent "style" out of what in reality is quite uneven.
I know it would be counterproductive for me to try to stand
my life still long enough to get everything lined up uniformly
and consistently. And I can't help thinking the same would be
true for people reading the book — even if the roughness
makes the book less "pleasant" to read. I even think that the
kind and tone of voice I use in different places can help people understand how deeply or superficially I was involved in
what I was writing — at least that is what comes to me when
I read back through what I have written.

Part 1

Experience

2

The Meaninglessness of Words

Words have little meaning. That is something we all know —
consciously or intuitively. That is part of the problem that I
talked about in the first chapter. Why write a book when so
much evidence points to the destruction of word meaning,
when ideas have degenerated into verbal games. There are
many ways to say that words have lost meaning; mostly we
are familiar with them — consciously or intuitively.

There is Orwellian meaninglessness — unthink and doublethink. The political rhetoric of our time is increasingly Orwellian. War is peace. Violence must be "controlled" with "overwhelming force." In Vietnam, the village of Ben Tre is bombed

to rubble in order to "protect" the inhabitants; a special forces camp is overrun and more than 150 Vietnamese and Americans are killed but the information officer claims a great victory since the purpose of the camp was to locate the enemy — a task which it has obviously fulfilled.

There is the meaninglessness of sheer volume. Clarity is strangled by the speed and massiveness of communication, the exposure of the individual to far more information than he can ever hope to sort or comprehend. And in the presence of such volume, precision and purpose in communication are difficult to keep track of; words are used carelessly by everyone; how could they be used any other way when they are obviously so cheap? And the perception that words are cheap and meaningless creates a blankness in us that important words cannot penetrate; we fail to hear the attempts by other people to speak to us. And since we are insensitive to the serious language that we are offered, we fail to learn how to speak seriously to others. During moments of self-awareness we realize that our own words are hollow, that we are talking to hear ourselves talk. We have "verbal diarrhea"; it is a contagious disease in our society — and almost everyone suffers.

There is the social-psychological meaninglessness of words. More and more people are aware of the fact that in small groups the content of what people say is unimportant and almost arbitrary. What is really going on is a game (called "group dynamics") in which what is important is who talks to whom, who leads, who follows, who supports, who conflicts. In reality what is happening is people trying to cope with a group; the words are simply a lubricant of social interaction, an indicator that helps people place one another in a social matrix. For example, classrooms communicate not ideas or concepts but instead a respect for academic authority, a distrust of our own emotive and intuitive responses, a belief that repressed apprenticeship to incomprehensible academic disciplines is legitimate and reasonable.

There is the media meaninglessness of words. The medium *is* the message. What we "read" when we pick up a book is not the words that are in it but an unconscious pattern of "linear" thought that is inherent in the written construction of language. Our entire way of thinking is shaped by the dominant media of our time through the unconscious implantation of their forms in our minds. And in an age of instant, electronic communication, we too become wired; man is remade in the image of a television set.

Finally, there is the meaninglessness of the meaninglessness. The social-psychological description of the emptiness of our words offers a false insight — the sense that we can trust our distrust — the sense that the words that say that words say nothing say truth. But like other truths, it belongs on the truth heap for we can do little with it. The very classrooms that inform us that the medium is the message continue to be like any other classrooms, authoritarian in structure and academic in tone. The group dynamist who reveals to us the mysteries of small group functioning is not interested in re-creating content in communication but in making us masters of group process. Meanwhile, the newspapers go on being newspapers, the TV, TV — the medium is transcendent. The volume of words grows exponentially. And Orwell seems more than ever a prophet: 1984 is now. In the end, the whole tirade of descriptions about the meaninglessness of words is a kind of unthink. In the name of cleansing our minds of their old habits of irrational communication, it leaves nothing. It restores no meaning to words; it leaves them broken and useless — like everything else, beyond our control. Our domination by alien language is complete; our submission to senseless, purposeless communication is reasonable; anything else would be quixotic. If in the beginning we were angered by the destruction of language, we must eventually come to the conclusion that our anger is futile, that there is nothing else to do but celebrate our helplessness; it is meaningless to worry about meaning.

Words have meaning. Consciously or intuitively, everyone knows that to be true.

It is no longer the task, if it ever was, to convince people that communication has been perverted. People know — even without being told. We read the newspapers with suspicion, if not disgust; we watch the tube (even the "cultural" programs) with a firm sense that beyond our superficial resistance, the thing grips our nervous systems and rots our minds. An eminent professor at Berkeley complains that even his brightest students have lost "faith" in the efficacy of rational, rigorous intellectual discourse. But the professor gives no reason why their faith should be sustained — in fact he seems passive and confused by this "disturbing trend." We are turned off by most groups we have contact with and see them as somebody else's ego trip; we recognize that most of what people say is bullshit. But we can offer no alternative. Like everyone else, we observe and participate in the destruction of language and word meaning. Somehow, we have given up the effort to rise above it.

If there is a need, it is not to convince people that words are meaningless. We already are too defeated by that knowledge. Rather it is to make people trust the fact that they can talk and believe in the possibility that they might have something to say, to convince them that the paradoxes of misinformation and misapprehension do not satisfactorily or totally describe human communication. Human communication does take place — significant, clear, forceful, cogent, relevant talk happens to all of us — although not very frequently and almost never in the places where it is *supposed* to. Occasionally people leave a classroom deeply provoked or shaken. Occasionally something in a newspaper or magazine wrenches us loose — although usually that something is an item that shouldn't have been there — something that slipped through the cultural censors, that stands out against the pap and slogans, something that is the more profoundly right because it can still be seen, imbedded as it is in the wrong place. Occasionally there is a meeting and people really talk to one another. Occasionally the message transcends the medium.

But usually communication we can trust happens in what we describe as the personal milieu. It is between me and a friend after a long absence and a couple of drinks and a long pause that the bullshit stops and the talk begins. Or it is profoundly not in the same situation when we could have, should have talked — were all around it, on the edge of it, but failed in the end to broach the subject that was there to be awakened, let it slip away, let ourselves slip away from each other without differentiating our contact from the undifferentiated contact with hundreds of others we had met and missed that day.

We talk to people; not enough; not frequently enough to satisfy the hunger for contentful communication, but it happens to all of us and should be part of the hard, trusted bedrock of our experience. The talk need not be profound (although it is that kind of breakthrough experience that rushes to my mind when I think of significant communication); it can be perfectly matter-of-fact, ordinary — unique because it is simple, because despite the pressure to be something else (to be a social game or a status symbol or a sexual gambit) it is simply what it is: three people planning a meeting or two people trying to understand a math problem. Or it can be matter-of-fact *and* something else.

For example, solving math problems was also once for me the first way of knowing a girl whom I tutored for a few weeks in college. The math was both a problem and the beginning metaphor of a relationship between two people, but, and this is important, it was somehow *quite explicitly both things* for both of us. Learning what prevented us from learning math opened a door to learning about each other. It was perhaps the only time that either of us enjoyed math and let the interplay of problem and personal metaphor goad us into taking

the time to comprehend how we reasoned mathematically
and why we had difficulty doing so. I suppose this sounds
awkward, but *it* was not; rather *we* were — young, awkward,
ill at ease with the social/sexual games that had been established
for us to play, tremendously relieved to find a situation of our
own creation that still provided the ambiguity for us to know
one another.

The communication we value is personal; it has very little
to do with the networks and elaborate structures and conventions of social communication — unless it can be described as
resistance to them, the intuitive assertion that the personal
milieu which the conventions wear down still has strength
and a kind of primacy. Yet despite its importance to us, the
absolute need we have to experience personal communication
and have it refreshed in order to protect our sanity and continue to function, we are not very assertive about it. The
society teaches us to question its validity; instructors frown
upon it or mock someone who would dare to introduce personal experience as "evidence." There is constant pressure to
isolate its meaning and deny its significance. If I understand
anything that this country wants me to understand, it is that I
should be embarrassed to talk about taking math and a woman
together; it is indecent exposure; it is either perverse or trivial
or both, or, to be gentle about it, it is one of those pleasant,
private memories to be nostalgic about in my next equally insignificant and nostalgic encounter with an old friend.

From a certain vantage point, this may be true. For part of
our joy in the relationship was its privateness, our separation
and insularity. But it is precisely that — privateness, separation,
insularity — that this society cannot stand. It is the insistence
that all communication, whenever and wherever it takes place,
must be socially monitored, saturated with status markers,
sublimated sexual inducements, competition, esoteric ritual and
structural reference that makes talk meaningless. And it is ultimately subversive to the whole social order to suggest that

personal criteria of validity might be substituted for the existing ones. For us to acknowledge to one another (with some embarrassment, to be sure) that the words that make sense to us are the words the society and all of its agents consider irrelevant and unimportant, is the beginning of a terrible and dangerous conspiracy.

Largely, I think of what I have said so far as self-evident, as intuitively clear. However, part of what I am concerned about is that seemingly self-evident ideas are so quickly discounted and discredited — that they so seldom become the basis of action or a shared vision or identity. That is what I mean when I say the society teaches us to question the validity of our own insights and experience, strips their meaning away from them and isolates them (and us).

For middle-class, college-educated folk who read this kind of book, one of the chief mechanisms for stripping away meaning is to make them grovel in front of meaningless profundities, to dance around the old truth heap, guarded as it is by bevies of sages and pundits and above all by experts. Our own awe at the wisdom of people we can't understand keeps us in line. It is more out of self-defense than to add anything to the above argument that I want to turn my attention to some of those profundities. It is only if we reduce some of their equations to our size (my math background comes in handy here) that we can hope to break away from our deep-seated affection for esoteric banality.

The people who say that words lack meaning have presumably put us in their debt. They have discovered that the social structures that control language and the media that transport it tend to override the "content" of communication. Media themselves, not their content, we are told, are what count. All of this wisdom is a paradox of sorts; what people think they are saying and hearing and what actually gets "said" and "heard" are two different things. It is this paradox that

provides the plot line for all the media theorists; we are all intrigued to know how it is that what we thought we were saying and hearing all these years suddenly turns out to be something else. In addition, we are angered a little to have been
taken in for so long and a wee bit envious of smart guys like
Marshall McLuhan who can brag in the introduction to *Understanding Media* that seventy-five percent of the material in his
book is new and imply that most of us, steeped as we are in
conventional wisdom and bigotry, won't be able to grasp it.
But suppose the paradox, when examined, wasn't that impressive. Suppose it turned out that all of us had "understood" it
and experienced it from before we could remember. Then
what?

   In fact, I think this is the case. The "great paradox" is not
so great; most of us do understand it, at least intuitively, and
cope with it all the time. I think that Edgar Friedenberg states
the guts of the paradox in *The Vanishing Adolescent*. He is
talking about how we learn to speak:

> The child who says there are big rats in the alley and gets
> spanked for lying the third time he says it learns something
> about how adults use language and the importance they attach
> to it. He learns what a spanking is and what a rat is not; all this
> is presumably useful knowledge to take along on the solitary
> journey toward maturity. But he does not learn, and neither
> do his parents, what he meant when he said there were rats in
> the alley. This gets plowed under.
>
>   The important point is not that we learn to talk in child-
> hood, but that we learn to repress meanings that are not sub-
> ject to consensual validation; we learn to keep quiet about
> what other people cannot see. . . . we learn in childhood to
> sacrifice emotional vividness to intellectual cogency.

   Probably Friedenberg should say "social cogency" rather
than "intellectual cogency," but the point is the same; growing

up can be seen as the filtering of the raw, animal, instinctual stuff that is a child through a social screen. A battle ensues and a lot, presumably a lot that is emotionally vivid and beautiful, gets plowed under. Learning to use the society's definition of "rat" (forgetting what we saw in the alley) is a mixed blessing. It allows us to communicate with other people, but it ties us to the social conventions and forms of communication; it makes us its subjects. Those conventions work on us; they define us, shape us, reduce us, mold us, make us into creatures that are fit to work for General Motors, to napalm villages, cripple one another through competitive games, and take joy from the ingenious, poetic way a child puts words together.

All of us are involved in resisting those conventions — more or less. (Friedenberg, I take it, feels that a measure of a good society is the amount of resistance it encourages in its young to the passive acceptance of its institutions and conventions.) We may long since have forgotten that remarkable thing we saw in the alley, but there is still the residue of a memory, a sense that what we saw (see) is right (real) and that what the society calls a "rat" is really a misshapen set of fears, prejudices and taboos that damages us and limits our potential. So we fight back — more or less. We fight our parents or schools, try to keep the job from destroying our spirit, don't believe the newspapers, get turned off by the group, start cutting classes, stop going to the lecture series.

It is never that words are meaningless. It is rather "our" meaning versus "their" meaning, a sense that words are filled with meaning, but that it is the wrong meaning — it is meaning we do not control or shape, cannot influence or mold, expand or contract. And it is not just the wrong words, it is very profoundly the wrong language. Existing political language is worse than cliché — it is banal, wretched, numbing — perfect for what it must do, which is make everybody hate politics. "New" political language is frantic, sectarian, impenetrable.

Academic language doesn't deserve comment. We suspect that TV might not be better with better programming; it might just be more insidious. The new wave of movies is already too slick, self-conscious, redundantly satiric, déclassé, involuted. The last time you were in the country (when was that?) you were actually frightened by what a dark night is like (completely dark) and realized that in your world the lights never go out, never stop working on you.

It is on this score that the media theorists offer a false truth. Because they all promise, directly or indirectly, that if we could understand their theories we would see through the problem of meaninglessness and be able to get some leverage on it. All the media theorists, from Orwell to McLuhan, agree on the nature of the problem. They contend that we do not understand the language we are using, do not recognize its actual structure. Our hope for liberation depends on comprehending that actual structure. The illusion is that once we understand the nature of political double-talk we will no longer be taken in; or once we recognize the way the printed word organizes our thought process, our minds will be unbent. And these seem like powerful truths to pursue. What the media theorists will help us do is master alien language; or taken as a whole, they will help us master the many alien languages that constitute our environment.

But here is the trap. The master of an alien language no longer considers it alien. He now considers it his own. The difference between master and slave is not that one is tied to an alien system and the other is not; the difference is that the master has forgotten that the system is alien; he now calls it his own; he now calls oppression, freedom. The slave at least knows that he is being beaten.

What happens is that the people who "discovered" and studied small-group process now become the authors of the science of small-group manipulation. Or better yet, Marshall McLuhan sets himself up in business to show modern corporations how they can really be modern, so that Marshall and the corporations can all make higher profits. Or closer to home, we see our more academically oriented and successful friends (or perhaps ourselves) beginning to slip into the cultured sterility of intellectual parlor games. Or the New Left, that learned all about political double-talk and mystification and promised to create a political vocabulary we could use, reaches the remarkable alien climax where it cannot put one sentence together straight. Mastering alien systems is not the way out. It is the way in. The way out begins with the recognition that all of *their* language is alien. The way out begins with the recognition that there is only one language we can properly be masters of — our own. The way out begins with the recognition that what is left of our language is what we have left of the truth as we are capable of knowing it. The rest belongs on the truth heap.

3

The Meaninglessness of Experience

It should be obvious that what I have called "words" or language refers to our *experience* of using words and language and having them used against us, and that our search for authentic language or communication is a search for authentic experience. And it should be equally clear, at an intuitive level, that the society is constantly pressing *its* meaning of *our* experience on us, and making us deny what we have felt. The process in which the society constantly reinterprets and socializes experience leaves us very little space.

Perhaps it is unnecessary to point out that our "ordinary experience" at school or on the job, in "social settings" such as parties and dances, is used against us. At one level, at least, it is obvious we don't have a chance in those situations; the social sanctions are very much up front and in the open — and they are very powerful — grades, money, promotions, social acceptance being the "positive" ones; derision, castigation, humiliation, economic and social insecurity being the negative.

But despite their force, we are all involved, more or less, in resisting those sanctions — we are involved, more or less, consciously or intuitively, in trying to make "our" meaning stand out against "theirs."

Let me try to illustrate from my own experience. I went to a school, Oberlin College, that had a thing called "academic pressure." No one was quite sure where it came from — whether it was the instructors who introduced it, or the students in their competitiveness with one another for grades, or whether it was just some mysterious quality of the institution that hung over everybody. But wherever it came from, most people were quite confident it was real. And that was some sort of advantage because at least there was no pretense, as there is in so many situations, that pressure (oppression) did not exist. I felt it, and felt it strongly enough to decide to try to resist it. I determined after one semester at the place that I was no longer going to have my life directed by grades, the bench mark of academic pressure. And for a whole year, until I wound up on academic probation and found it necessary to reconsider my stand, I didn't look at my grades. For a year I congratulated myself (felt above my fellow students) for having shaken the grading system and impressed my friends by telling them I didn't know what I'd gotten on the latest exam. I tried to convince myself that I was involved in "learning for its own sake," but in retrospect it's clear (and I can barely convince myself that it wasn't clear then) that there was very little, if anything, in any of my courses that actually held my interest — save perhaps tutoring in math. I created, in place of grades, a kind of academic appetite, a "thirst for learning," that

was as dilettantish and distant from me as it was dull and hard
to pursue (thence the probation). I plowed through reading
lists with stupid methodicalness, bought and underlined the first
half of books, took verbatim notes, and turned out reams of
pseudo-academic prose. And of course, I was still quite conscious of how my teachers were grading me. I knew which
ones had had high hopes for me and were disappointed in my
performance. I knew which ones were pleased with my work
— and why — and I performed for them with stellar con-
sistency — all in the name of "learning for its own sake."

But the most important thing to note here is that in the
courses I did actually manage to become absorbed in, I believe
I really wanted to know how my teachers graded me. That is
to say, I still mightily needed recognition, acknowledgment
and approval from someone; I could not make the academic
myth of inner-direction and self-sufficiency work. And if my
professors' evaluation of my work was different from mine, I
needed to argue that they were wrong and I was right. And
on those few occasions when I actually wrote something I
really felt was good, I needed to demand recognition of its
goodness — and if I didn't get it, I wanted bloody well to
scream at the professor, "That's Me you just marked D plus.
You can't mark Me D plus. No one gave you the right to mark
Me anything. That's Me. See. So get your dirty marks off Me
and let Me grow." But of course I was afraid to do that. And
of course what I told myself was that I didn't care about grades.

It's pretty clear that what I'd done, a little bit before it
became voguish to demand it as an academic reform, was to
prove that grades are not that necessary as an inducement to
get people to bury themselves under the old truth heap. Grades
have their place of course. But at an institution like Oberlin,
they really are unnecessary. All that is really necessary is to
turn the students loose and they will devour themselves.

I mention this example because it seems to me typical. Most
of us try to resist or buffer ourselves against the raw power of

the social sanctions we come up against. Characteristically our resistance is personal because we perceive that other people around us have adapted to the pressure that defeats us. This perception, when you think about it, is almost as arrogant as it is self-deprecating: it forces us to view other people as insensitive or unaware. And equally characteristic, our resistance turns in upon us; we repudiate one of the sanctions of the system (grades) by internalizing one of its higher values ("thirst for knowledge"). Our rebellion is used to create (and is frequently done in the name of) a higher allegiance to the system. If it succeeds (had I shaken the grading system), it can be used to show that the system really does work (that students who really do partake of the search for knowledge can discard grades without in any way injuring the system). And if it fails (which it did), it can usually be described as a personal failure ("He really wasn't ready to strike out on his own") and therefore a justification for the use of the sanctions in the first place. The circle is closed. There is no exit.

But way back at the beginning, there was something else. There was a very profound feeling that things were wrong — that Oberlin wasn't turning out at all to be what I wanted it to be, that my experience there was just as corralled and stifled as it had been in high school — maybe even worse. When I looked around for an explanation of my dissatisfaction, the system had already provided the answer — academic pressure. My rebellion had already been programmed. When I wound up on probation, I finally admitted that my rebellion had failed, that for some reason which I really didn't understand I did not want to flunk out, that grades were important, and that I would have to pursue them. It was an acknowledgment that the system was too powerful for me and that I was much too loyal to it to contemplate a complete break. And even though I was active in campus politics and reform movements, by the second semester of my sophomore year I had been beaten, and a half-forgotten ache that I carried all through my Oberlin career never quite let me forget it. My defeat (my loyalty) made my politics a kind of half-lie. It was only late in my senior year when my degree was already assured, had already begun to collect dust in my imagination, that I remembered the feeling that had gotten lost somewhere back before I made the decision not to pay any attention to grades. And when I remembered it I started crying, not only out of knowledge of what had been lost, but out of the deep recognition that my life had prepared me for nothing but losing it again.

But there are other settings in which our experience has a better chance, where the contest between "us" and "them" is not so heavily weighted against us. I have talked about private and personal examples of that experience in the previous chapter. But there are also occasions, not frequently, perhaps only a few times in a lifetime, perhaps never in reality but only in fantasy, when we have an experience that I can only describe as a breakaway experience or a revolutionary experience. It is an experience that shatters the distinction between "private" and "public" experience, an authentic experience that is emphatically social in all its implications but reaches down to the very bottom of our personal sense of identity and reshapes it. I call it revolutionary because it has the capacity to break us decisively away from our past, but also because so much of it has been created by the thing we call the movement, even though it does not have to happen in that milieu or to result from the conscious attempt to create a breakaway experience. It can happen anytime, anyplace, to anyone. It happened to me when I was eight, completely unexpectedly, when I suddenly found myself screaming at my parents at the supper table that I was tired of hearing them bicker and quarrel. They were both startled beyond recognition of me, because I had never screamed at either of them before, and suddenly there I was, right in the middle of a very ordinary, everyday, minor quarrel, acting like a maniac. I don't believe either of them had the faintest idea what was happening — and they were unusually perceptive parents. But as I ran out of the room crying I think I realized that my scream had said more about what I felt for them — how deeply I shared their pain and unhappiness, how passionately I still loved them — than I had ever said before — or for that matter have ever said since. But it was a break-away experience. I had finally given voice to my anger at what they were doing to me, and although my voice frightened me terribly, I recognized it as my own. In my memory that experience stands out as the the first point at which I understood that I was not willing to live in my parents' world, the point at which I began to understand that my life had to be radically separated from theirs.

But even this kind of vivid, breakaway experience can be reinterpreted and undermined and inverted by this society. I am certain that I later felt guilty about my outburst against my parents — even as I tried to hang on to some of its meaning. And it is that I want to talk about here. I want to talk about how the society comes eventually to use even our most important breakaway experiences against us. And as an example of that, I want to talk about the 1968 Democratic National Convention in Chicago, show how it was a revolutionary experience for me and other people who were there, and show how it has been (is being) undermined and turned against the people who were most affected by it.

One reason for using the Chicago example is because what happened there became a rather celebrated event, and I suppose if you wanted to find the roots of the trouble with that experience you would have to start with the media attention that was focused on it. Because everybody, all over the country, got a look at what was going on there, and they all had their ideas about what was happening and their fantasies about what it must have been like to be there. So when people went away from Chicago and tried to talk about it, other people already had strong ideas about what it meant. But I'm getting ahead of my story. First I should try to say what it was like to be there, and then I will tell the story of how it got changed.

I'm not sure why people came to Chicago. There were no doubt lots of different sets of reasons. But almost everybody knew, by the time they got there, that Chicago was an armed camp. The papers were filled with it; how could they help but be? Mayor Daley was putting together a force that could have repulsed the proverbial invasion from the Asian mainland. So one of the first things you brought with you into the city was this sense of an incredible force being arrayed against you. But for most people coming into town, even for me working in the Mobilization Committee office for two weeks before, we just couldn't quite get it through our heads that all of that force was being lined up against us. It was too abstract; it was too absurd.

The first day really did nothing to change that image. There were a lot of people hanging around in Lincoln Park in a bizarre setting since bunches of cops were milling around too, but nothing much happened except an unorderly, noisy, pleasant but uneventful march downtown to picket the Convention hotels.

But then that night people got chased out of the park by the cops at eleven and it started to happen. And if you think about it, the event itself didn't seem that important. It wasn't as if anybody was surprised that we got chased out of the park because everybody knew that was going to happen. It was right on the schedule so to speak. But of course people felt it wasn't right that we couldn't stay in the park, so they stayed around until eleven o'clock to make sure the cops had to chase us out of the park and to show that we didn't think they had a right to chase us out — but knowing all along that they would, definitely, chase us out.

And they did. We ran into the streets of Old Town, maybe a couple of thousand of us at the most, which was the first thing that happened that only a few people had really thought that much about. People were standing around in the streets and on the sidewalks. There was a lot of noise coming from everywhere, especially back in the park where some people were still being pushed out by the cops. Traffic was starting to get jammed up a little and the streetlights and the neon after the utter darkness of the park put a funny color on everything. Then the cops started clearing off the streets and some people ran around a lot, but most people just stood around and got pushed back by the cops, and once in awhile you heard rumors that somebody had been hit or hurt or something had happened, but you really didn't see much — just what I've described. And that was it. Or at least that was the beginning of it.

What had happened outwardly was that a bunch of people had gotten pushed around by a bunch of cops. Nothing very unusual about that. It happens every day to thousands of people. But inwardly, what had happened to a lot of people sometime between leaving the park and leaving Old Town was that they had understood somehow that they were locked into this thing with the cops (and there was even a sense that it was a kind of drama — though real drama), and that this was just the beginning of it and that it was going to go on and get worse and be very ugly. A lot of it was in the faces of the cops, who were really scared and full of hate, marching up and down in Old Town, tearing ass off in twenty directions in their vans with blue lights flashing. But some of it was in us. Us as a group of people who had just been pushed around by cops. Us as this funny set of occupants of the street. But, us also as this really variegated set of people who nonetheless looked more like each other than anybody else. It wasn't just the cops that brought us together, it was all those people driving by in cars peering out at us, or the people sight-seeing in Old Town, just like us, looking around trying to figure out what was going on, but so different. They were all leading very normal lives, going to Old Town, and they'd run into this strange happening, this bunch of people out in the street shouting and looking weird. Or they couldn't move their cars so they could get back to Evanston so they were a little pissed, but since they all had dates and things, they couldn't be too pissed or it would look like they were losing their cool. So mainly they just sort of looked around or tooted their horns once in awhile, which just made it noisier. Maybe it was just those curious people, most of all, that made us understand that they were in some sort of different world.

The idea spread that we were involved in this thing with the cops until I think pretty much everybody was involved in it. That's what people talked about most — how it was going to go with the cops. And even though you could find lots of people who would say that the cops were going to cool it at the last minute just like they're always supposed to, nobody put too much stock in it, even the people who were arguing for it. People couldn't figure out any rational reason why they wouldn't let us march to the amphitheater. We were just a few thousand people — we could easily be contained — we really couldn't storm the amphitheater with all the troops. But that's like sitting around and wondering why the U.S. doesn't get out of Vietnam — since it so easily could. You can argue that there's no rational reason why it shouldn't, but that doesn't deal with the problem that it doesn't and "can't." We were beginning to understand that the level of rationality operating in Chicago just couldn't conceive of us marching to the amphitheater or sleeping in the park. And this was the correct observation because it suggested that "our" level of rationality and "theirs" had drifted so far apart that we just couldn't even guess at what theirs was any more.

Meantime, we were all getting a commitment to stay. Lots of people had come there just to look in, very uncertain about the whole venture and the groups sponsoring it. But they kept getting pulled in, and of course each night it was getting a little bit more violent, because the cops had started really going after people in the streets. It's really important to understand why people got sucked into it and why they decided to stay and how they exchanged whatever commitment they had come with for this funny sense that they had to stick it out. Because on paper, up in the police chief's office, I'm sure it said that severe police tactics were supposed to discourage people from risking their necks. But as in so many cases the tactics were having the opposite effect. The uglier things got, the more people got this determination about staying. I think what kept people there was the fact that it was a real drama, that what was happening in Chicago, if you pulled back the skin just a little bit, was what was really happening all over America. The gulf of complete incomprehension growing throughout the country had already led to the decision by the people who make decisions that we had to be destroyed — and if Mayor Daley took the decision a little bit more literally than did more sophisticated tacticians, it didn't mean that he had misunderstood the issue or the decision.

The pigs understood. The pigs were very ideological; they realized we were this terrible social disease and that they were a moral force that had to stop it. They weren't confused for a moment into thinking that their job was to *maintain* law and order. They were much more righteous than that. They knew their job was to defend their country and their morality, and that meant striking out against this plague that had come into the country and the city.

We knew that we just couldn't give in to that morality. We knew that if we couldn't look straight at the naked truth about America and the certainty of the violence that would be used if they couldn't find some other way to smother us, and keep right on going in the grip of that violent truth, then we'd just as well give it all up right then and there. So the question was whether or not we could survive against all those peering, peeping, club-swinging, hating, incomprehending, manikin-like people. Somehow it had never come through quite like that before. We'd all talked about struggle and conflict and the crimes of this country against humanity, but somewhere in the backs of our minds we'd all had the sense that the country could go right on committing those crimes and we could go right on being part of it — that is, protected by it in some sense. Protected not from jeers and funny looks and raised eyebrows in personnel offices, but protected from the most brutal, wanton, murderous side of it. And then, all of a sudden, there we were looking at it, the bared teeth, the hatred and the overwhelming force. Everything about the situation was true and real, even though, as I've said, it was a drama. It was clear that we couldn't hope to defeat the force they had, so what we had to do was look after our own skins and those of our friends and our comrades in the street, but we had to stay there and do that. We had to prove to ourselves and them and everybody that we could survive in Chicago in the face of their repressive apparatus. And we did survive. That was the most important experience and lesson that we got from Chicago — that we could survive in America no matter what they tried to do to us.

There were two things involved in that. First was the understanding that we *had* to survive, which for middle-class people, which most of us were, is a pretty incredible leap. Always before, as I said, we carried this false sense of security, this policemen-are-my-friends notion that the society would buffer us in some way, and I suppose that implies as well a deep fear of doing anything that would tear away that buffer. But the buffer was gone in Chicago and you realized, perhaps, that maybe the buffer had never been there at all and that in some sense it was by sheerest circumstance that you'd never wound up on this side of the fence before. In a flash, like that, it all came home to roost, that we were in danger and had to learn how to defend ourselves and look out for one another. By defend I don't mean learning how to fight cops; defense meant learning how to run in a group so that nobody got lost or left behind where the pigs could corner them and beat the shit out of them; defense meant learning how to help one another resist panic, and how to talk about fear. Of course when people got a chance to get back at the cops they did, but that really wasn't very important, because all of us knew the cops had almost all the force. The second part of survival, after you learned you had to worry about it, was doing it — and that turned out to be much easier than we might have expected if we'd just thought about it abstractly because the really important thing was that there were people all around you who were doing it and you weren't alone. Fighting when you're not alone, even if you're outnumbered and outweighed, can be okay. What comes out of that is the sense that we are potentially a powerful resource for one another.

The second great lesson/experience of Chicago was the discovery that we were all yippies. To paraphrase Dick Gregory, if you were in the streets and if you moved, you were a yippie. The cops had decided that, and it didn't make a tinker's dam to the cops whether you had a beard and sandals or a McCarthy button and a tie, whether you were pursuing the "correct political line" or wanted desperately just to have a nice, non-violent peace parade, whether you were standing with your hands in your pockets or had just thrown a rock through a cruiser windshield. If you were on the street you were a yippie. By the end of the week, we'd begun to realize that it was true, began to understand, perhaps for the first time in our lives, what it really means to be objectified. What we were learning was that if this society says you are something (a yippie), it doesn't make any difference what you think you are, you *are* a yippie. What we were learning must be similar to what is driven home in black communities every time there is an uprising. Because when the racist pigs come storming into your community with their guns and their fear and their hatred, if you're black you're the enemy. It doesn't make any difference whether you've been downtown trying to make it right with the man or whether you know somebody at the war on poverty — if you're black you're the enemy — if you're on the street, you're a yippie. And by god, after just about three days of it, you are.

That process, if you'll recall, had started on the first night — when up in Old Town people had begun to look at one another and understand how they *were* the same — in that vague

sense of being more like one another than the people around us
— the understanding that we shared something important, just
by virtue of being there and being able to recognize one another. It really cut through — for me, and I think for many
people there — a lot of the sectarian shit that the Movement
carries around in its normal defensive, precarious mood. I even
felt good about the McCarthy kids coming over to Grant Park
after we'd liberated it, even though the day before they'd been
doing everything they could to climb in bed with the Democratic party, because I thought the message was so strong that
even the McCarthy kids would realize that out in the park they
were yippies. If they didn't understand it right off, the pigs,
who were very patient, would teach them. And sure enough,
the very next night when a bunch of McCarthy people tried
to have a march, they blasted them. However, a lot of people
did get upset to see the McCarthy people coming in, I guess
because they felt "we" had won the battle and deserved credit
for it. But I still had, up to the very end, this very strong
feeling that it was the sheerest circumstance that had enrolled
any of us in this very powerful experience, and that anybody
who went through it, regardless of their previous political
orientation, would have to come out with the same understanding. In retrospect that seems optimistic, but at the time I knew
it was correct.

So that was the revolutionary, breakaway experience of
Chicago, and I have taken time to tell it because it is a complicated experience and also because I think the things we
learned are worth telling in their own right. You must understand that when I left Chicago, the feeling of that experience
was very vivid in my mind, although I had only begun to get
words to describe it. So I kept telling people we were all
yippies, but couldn't quite explain it. And you of course will
want to know how an experience — if it is that vivid and that
close and that revolutionary and that dramatic — can slip away.
   It is very easy. The first thing you realized when you got

home and started to explain was that you'd got this completely new frame of reference which your friends didn't understand, and maybe you got this sinking feeling (I know I had it) that they weren't going to understand. I think it was our friends, not our enemies, who were the first to help us undermine our experience, because we were so anxious for them to understand, and yet so completely without knowledge of how to communicate this new sense of ourselves.

People wanted to know what we thought the demonstrations had accomplished, meaning how did we think they had changed the current political scene or something. It seemed like such a logical question that we were a little bit startled to discover that we hadn't really thought that much about it. Because we hadn't really thought of accomplishments; we'd thought about survival or getting through in one piece. But it's that kind of question — What did you accomplish? — which, if you're politically oriented, as were most people who came to Chicago, you feel you ought to be able to answer. It is a comment on the limitations of the current political climate that we felt it would be unacceptable to answer that what the demonstrations had accomplished was to completely turn our heads around. Sometimes when I tried to say something like that, I choked up because I was afraid people were going to think I'd flipped. I mean what would you have said if a friend of yours came back from Chicago and said that what had happened was he'd discovered we are all yippies?

I suppose before I go any further, it's worth pointing out, if it isn't obvious already, that it is, most generally, our friends who help us deny the validity of our experience. Because on the whole, the level of communication we have with our friends isn't that deep or probing. What it is, more than that, is reassuring and comforting, and god knows, all of us, when we came back from Chicago or from any real experience, needed some reassurance. We get into these very complicated patterns of relating with our friends that provide a sort of nervous comfort, and we get our own language and our own styles of moving together, all of which reassure us in the way a fence reassures a farm animal, with the important difference that it's a big field and you usually don't even see the fence, just know somehow that it's there, guarding the borders. If a breakaway experience implies anything, it implies that you might cross that fence and leave some or all of your friends behind, and that's just a plain scary thought. So you get involved in a kind of conspiracy of silence.

Of course the other side of that is when one of your friends does get involved in a breakaway experience, and really does stand aside and make an announcement that she has changed, and is willing to make an invidious distinction between herself and you — is willing to separate herself — then that is a terribly liberating experience, because in fact you can use that person's experience to measure your own against. If I could have come back from Chicago and said straight out that I was a yippie, and not apologized for it but said I was glad to be a yippie, or if not glad, willing to be a yippie; if that is what it had come to, then my friends could have either just decided that I was completely crazy and thrown me out in the cold, which of course was what I was afraid they'd do, or they could have taken the only other alternative that is really available when somebody makes that kind of statement, and looked very hard at what I was trying to get across, which means looking very hard at themselves and their own experience to see whether they had any way of comprehending what I was saying. Of course, when they looked, some people would have seen one thing and some people would have seen others, which would have meant that people would have to look at their relationships to one another as well as to me, which perhaps would have meant that we would have gotten a fresh start with one another. One of the most conscious cravings I have with most of my friends is for us to somehow get clear on one another (get clear *of* one another) so that we can see things with us as they really are and have been.

But for the purposes of this narrative and the idea I'm trying to get across about how breakaway experience, and other kinds of authentic experience, gets undermined by our friends, it's important to underscore that I did not stand aside, did not dare to make an invidious distinction between myself and my friends. I am not a weak person, and it was not a weak experience, which for me says a lot about how powerful are the forces we must overcome and how desperately we need help from the thing we call the movement in doing that.

Of course the media helped to fuck us up here, because the damned Convention had been so played up and the Democratic party had been so thoroughly exposed and seemed to be in such a shambles, and everybody was so shook up and running around, that everyone had the feeling that something had really changed. People thought the movement had got hold of some power that it had used in Chicago that it could actually use to change political events that were happening right then. We all had been involved in the media business at some level, had been aware that the drama that had been going on in Lincoln Park and Old Town had been played on national television one night, and that the "whole wide world had been watching." But we failed to think hard enough about the difference between *seeing* the drama and *being in* it, and therefore took our friends more seriously than we should have when they suggested that we had done a lot more than just get through it alive — which is another way of saying we took something away from the importance we had attached to having survived.

We didn't even have the good sense to believe in our own propaganda, which had said all along that the Democratic party was going to strangle itself in its own security, paranoia and rigidity. We actually began to believe that the Democratic party had tripped over, been tripped up by, us, rather than realizing that it had really only swallowed itself in its own slime. So there we were, just a few days after the Convention, trying to figure out the answer to the question of how we'd done it, trying to devise a strategy so that we could do it again, trying to learn how to create two, three, many Chicagos.

But of course none of us really "knew" how Chicago had happened, not even the people who had been most intimately involved in planning the demonstrations — maybe, most of all, not us. What we did know was that something important had happened to us while we were there, and it is certainly not a bad instinct to have wanted to think about how to create situations where that experience could be shared. But in order to have had any hope of doing that it would have been necessary for us really to work through what had happened to us, come to grips with and digest the knowledge that we had been changed, and prepare to meet the incomprehension our change was bound to be greeted with.

Right here, I suppose it's worth pointing out that the one thing that would have led most of us really to do hard, deep thinking about what we had just been through, and to trust our insights, would have been the presence of a movement that told people the revolution was inside *them,* inside their real and potential breakaway experience. We needed a movement that could help make it legitimate and right for people to think about and believe in the integrity of their experience. But the movement that existed basically believed that the revolution was not in us — but was out there, somewhere. And if we couldn't find support for believing in our own experience inside the movement, where else were we going to find it? Not anywhere else in the society where people were so busy swallowing themselves. Maybe a little trembling bit in ourselves, but not nearly enough to withstand the pressure to capitulate.

Already we were drifting away from the recollection of that experience, thinking instead about how we were to prevent the establishment from holding any public events until the war was over, planning to drive the election campaign underground, organizing boycotts and god knows what all.

Meanwhile there were things happening with people other than our friends. There were all those sympathetic liberal peo-

ple who'd been "shocked" at what they saw and were prepared
to hear about the barbarity of the police, but who had to be
reassured that we were really just good, decent, American kids
who'd been brutalized by the cops. So they kept asking whether
or not any of the demonstrators had been provocative, and
was it true that some of the demonstrators had actually thrown
bags of shit and piss like it said in the papers. The answer to
that, if there was an answer to a question that was so far out
of touch with what had actually happened, was that of course
we were provocative, that our very existence in America had
become a provocation, and that the pigs in Chicago were onto
that and were intent on destroying us, and that it doesn't make
a bit of difference one way or the other, when someone is
trying to destroy you, if you throw a bag of shit or not. But
the liberal people were as usual all caught up in this legalistic
sense of how the society operates and thought that if we had
just been standing there trying to peaceably assemble and the
cops had charged us, that would be one thing, a clear violation
of our rights and something to be angry about, but that if the
cops had just been standing there and one of us had thrown
a bag of shit, it would be another. Of course that's a very
moral, liberal, legalistic notion and is put forward with a lot of
self-righteousness, so that if you hadn't really thought through
your experience and got a grip on it, you were likely to forget
that the real provocation was that we were alive and fall right
back into this thing of trying to figure out who threw what
first — which, as I've said, didn't have anything to do with the
situation. But it was so hard to explain what had really happened that it was easy to slip back into arguing on the liberals'
terms, because it *was* clear that we had been on the defensive
and that it was the cops who kept pushing us around, so it
seemed as if you could win the argument on the liberals'
grounds without having to get a headache trying to explain
what really happened. But that lost sight of the fact that the
only thing worth fighting about with the liberals in the first

place was what ground to fight on. So we lost that battle whether or not we convinced the liberals that we weren't provocative.

On another level you had to start thinking about whether or not we were provocative, because after all it does seem a little bit melodramatic to say that they wanted to destroy us or that our existence was the provocation — and if you don't trust that insight, then you have to start looking for another explanation of how it all happened and you invariably get tangled up in bags of shit. This abandonment of a feeling for what had really happened also led people to accept the criticism that Chicago had "confused politics"; which was true of course, but was also irrelevant in terms of what had actually happened. By the time people got to the point of trying to think what the "correct politics" for Chicago might have been, they were too far out of touch with the experience to think well about what kind of political conception might have facilitated it.

Finally, people were undermined by the fact that when they got home, life just went merrily along, pretty much as it always had. And although most of us had to work at it, we managed to fit into it somehow. What else was there to do? Even if at times you saw a pig look at a kid full of hatred or felt all of a sudden that sense of precariousness you'd felt in Chicago, there was no place to go with the feeling.

The saddest thing of all is that occasionally I still hear people talking about Chicago, and it's as if it had never happened, as if nothing ever really happened there, as if it's just something that people made up to talk about like all the other things they make up all the time, just one more tiresome item on the tiresome agenda of tired political topics people make up to talk about.

Let me summarize what I have just said in a slightly different way. What I learned from Chicago was the strong, clear, con-

tradictory knowledge that revolutionary experience is possible
and impossible: that our lives are laced with examples of breakaway experience, some of them extraordinarily clear and vivid,
but that the society is completely geared up to isolate the
meaning of that experience and ultimately convert it into fantasy. Or to put it in the general language of the previous
chapter, the price extracted from us in exchange for the right
to use words (a language) and all the things that are attached
to them (most importantly self-consciousness) is the agreement
that we will help to obliterate the meaning of our own authentic experience. Quite simply, when we lose track of the beautiful, terrifying things that can be found in allies (things that
no society has ever been willing to look at), we lose track of
ourselves. What we preserve in whatever anger we have against
the society that shaped us is a faint memory of how much we
have been disfigured.

The experience of growing up is the experience of having
the society plant something deep down inside of you, almost
at the very bottom, that is not your own. Those incredible
things we call our minds do not really belong to us. They
belong to our parents and Oedipus and Richard Nixon and the
Pentagon and all the corporation presidents and most of all to
all the other poor mutilated creatures who loved us so much
that they trampled and crushed all the animal stuff that once
marked our potential so that we could be like them. Even our
neuroses are not our own. They belong emphatically to our
parents. What is ours (as much as anything can be) is anger
and humiliation and shame. What is ours is the sense of emptiness — a sense that we have been torn away from ourselves,
lost track of who we are, and in so doing, lost track of the
capacity to touch the other people around us. What is very
much ours is a terrible need to fill that emptiness.

Let me call that need the need for love.

4

Love

I want to make an assertion now, and I want to ask you to think about it as carefully as you can from your own experience to see whether or not you feel it is right. That is, I want you to ask the question, is this right for me and does it seem right for the people I know? The assertion is that what most Americans want more than any other thing is love. I know that this is not what a radical is supposed to say; I know I am supposed to say that Americans are crazed about possessions and power and status or material security, but it is my conviction that all of those things are secondary wants, that they are the things people eventually accept because they can't get love.

Or ask the question this way. What is it, the people you know really want out of life, what is it they're after, what exactly is it that people always seem to be chasing? And when I think about this question, the first thing that occurs to me is that some of the people I know, including myself, *are* chasing or once chased images of power and glory and prestige and were really fascinated and excited and strongly attracted to these images. But each year more of us begin to act as if we think those images have tarnished; and each year people realize those images are tarnished at an earlier age. Even the people I know who are striving in the good old American way to get ahead really don't seem to put so much stake in it and maybe even are a little bit embarrassed to admit that they have ambition to achieve. It's as if right under the surface of official American admiration for money and prestige people want something else. And I think that something is love, a desire to be whole and free. Or to say it another way, what I think the people I know want is love — even though they are supposed to want a Barracuda or a promotion and even though they themselves sometimes think they do.

As a matter of fact, the craving for love is so close to the surface as to be part of American folklore. The Baptist minister in the small farm town in Illinois where I grew up had a favorite sermon which he gave several times a year about the rich and prestigious man who died miserable. He managed to draw a moral, something like "rich people should go to church," but the point of the story was clear nonetheless; there is a widespread popular suspicion that "making it" will not solve "the problem." And even though the country is explicitly set up to allay this suspicion by rewarding people well for their competitive accomplishments, the suspicion hangs on and gets stronger. Each year, more and more Americans, in whatever way they express it, are beginning to catch on to the fact that this country isn't all it's cracked up to be, and whether you sweat your ass off in a factory or press your white collar in a computer, you know it. The problem, the thing that can't be satisfied, is our need for love — or that, at least, is what I think my friends would call it.

But whether they call it love or something else, I don't believe Americans think they can get it. There is another piece of American folklore about the resignation that signals maturity, the final, fatalistic peace that comes when a man realizes he will not accomplish his dreams. To be mature in this country is to know you won't find what you want, yet continue to play out your life. Growing up, after a point, is thought of as giving up, even though it is never portrayed that way. Giving up is always made to look like maturity. That is what you might call a bit of American realism.

So we have these two things: first that people want love; and second, that they don't think they can get it — even though not getting it in the end turns out to be "dignified." Taken together these two ideas constitute a fairly thorough condemnation of America, even though that is not what people talk about when they are condemning America. Somehow we would not think to say that the fact that people can't get what they want is a reason to condemn the country; it is much too direct and simple. Our conception of "politics" is much more oblique. But if you think about it, you will realize that accepting this notion that what we really want most is love has very important political implications. Our whole sense of what it is to be political and how to talk politically must be changed.

When I asked myself as honestly as I can, what is the thing I feel most broken and angry about, what do I really want most, the answer is love. And I believe that I am not alone. I believe that almost everyone I know is with me. But it is not something we talk about politically; it is not a subject that someone would bring up at an SDS meeting or any other kind of political gathering. In fact it is something we hardly talk about at all. It is too important. We are too confused about it.

We are too unsuccessful with it. We are not at all certain that it is real — and this is certainly understandable since love is nowhere. It has almost completely disappeared, if it ever was there, from the ugly, humorless, socioeconomic relationships our parents call marriage. And it is certainly not in any of those other places where it is talked about or portrayed — like movies or books or even poetry, although sometimes when poetry is set to music, it seems almost to be there. And it is not in all those places because it is most emphatically not in our own lives — none of our lives — no one's life; none of us know about it so none of us can say anything right about it. Oh, we are close; we are all around it; we have tasted it, touched it, caressed it in our dreams, but it has always eluded us. We have seen our friends stop looking for it, and we can only imagine when our parents stopped looking, and there is a little growing dead space inside us that tells us that someday we will stop looking too. The thing we want most is nowhere. In this society, love is impossible. In the end, we give it up for the other things, the hard stuff we can get, that at least comes packaged in sex/love symbols. But inside, if they are forced to stop to listen, Americans can still hear the hard stuff rattle in the awful cavity of hunger. And so long as people are hungry they will work. Right in behind their conscious quest for the things this society has to offer (possessions and power), Americans really are hungry for something they can't get. What a man wants from a Barracuda is a feeling he can't get. As a matter of fact, even if the Barracuda gets him what it is supposed to — sexuality and conquest — it still cannot fill up the depleted self-image that made him need to conquer in the first place. He is still basically empty (unfilled, unfulfilled, hungry) and some part of him knows it. Not all that long ago, people seemed to believe more deeply in the power of the Barracuda to do what it was supposed to; they were more absorbed in acquisitive dreams and images. But these days more and more people, some of them before they even begin the possessions quest, realize that a Barracuda can only entertain them for a few minutes before the hunger returns to gnaw away.

Long ago, so I'm told, hunger had to do with eating. Primitive man had to harness all his social energy to make a society that would give him enough food to keep from starving. But hunger today has nothing to do with eating. Even eating for most people has little to do with eating. Eating is to fill that new hunger that is so much bigger than the hunger for food — so women who are worried about being fat eat when they are unhappy. The food we put into our bodies has been perverted by that other hunger. And all our other simple appetites have been distorted and perverted as we seek new and more elaborate ways to satisfy the insatiable craving. If we call the hunger the need for love, and if we have a society in which the need for love can never be met, then we have a society in which men will work forever, even though their stomachs and all their other apparent needs were filled years ago.

But supposing we could find a way to liberate love. Supposing we could suddenly, one day, find a way for people to be what they want to be — whole and free and loving. Then the other hunger would stop and people could attend to their stomachs and other simple needs in the great tradition of their noble ancestors.

But what is this other hunger and where did it come from? The answer, if you think about it, is clear. It is a hunger for the residue of a memory that got plowed under. It is the hunger for an emotionally vivid, personal reality that got spanked and slapped and straightened and instructed until at last it seemed ephemeral and illusory. It is a hunger whose origins we were told to forget shortly after we first felt it which was shortly after we were born. It is a hunger that the society has taken over and promised to satisfy. The society calls it the hunger for power and property and status and security. Those are the names that will make us work the alien machinery they call civilization. They are false names. They are false gods. The name of the hunger is love. Love is God. God is love.

You will want to know what exactly it is I mean by love, because the way I have been talking so far suggests that what I mean by love is not necessarily what most people mean by love when they talk about it, but is something more abstract. And although I think the best way to understand what I mean to say is to try to understand it intuitively out of your own experience, I will try to be more clear. Because I will agree that the way I talk about love here is not the way we normally talk about love even though I think the two ideas are closely connected. On the few occasions when we do talk about love we usually talk about love for a specific person — some one person who we love or who loves us. Or more likely, we talk about love when the experience of trying to find love is so wrenching and twisting that we are forced to overcome our shyness about it and confide our pain in a close friend. That is the way we talk about love — quietly and intimately and specifically. Our talk about love is focused on the specific hope that the right woman (women) will come along, that everything will be easy and natural, that all the hidden constraint and unhappiness that marks our relationships with all people will at last be left behind with at least one person. (Just one person, to love and hold and cherish.)

But if you think about what that one specific woman is supposed to do for you, the way she is supposed to make you feel, you will realize that even our specific aspirations for love are for things that are quite abstract. What we fantasize we would feel — or what we have felt during those relatively brief moments when love has been alive for us — is something as abstract as wholeness or openness or peace. But even though these things are quite abstract, they are real, and their reality goes beyond something we want with just one person. Their reality describes what we want from life. So when I say that what we want most from life is love, I mean that what we want is to be whole and free. What we want is to find peace through overcoming the conflict between ourselves and others, to find a way to be open with at least one other person, even though that desire symbolizes our desire to be open with all of our world.

But to say that love described in these terms is impossible, is to say the obvious. It is so obvious that we never even think about the possibility that we could live in a world where deep love could be realized among many, many people. We are skeptical of our ability to find deep love with even one person, not to mention many. What we fail to understand is that our inability to find love with one person is precisely our inability to find love with many. What fucks us up in those few relationships we decide to attend to seriously and try to "make work," is exactly what allows us to have such brutal, distant relationships with everybody else.

What we want is love. Love is the most important thing. But we don't know how to talk about it. Not only do we not know how to talk about it; we don't even know how to think about it. To learn to think about love in a new way is to discover real cause and effect in our lives, is to look at the society and our action in it in a totally new way. I do not claim to have that new way of thinking about love. But I do have beginning images I think I can share — because I think they are shared.

5

Images of Love

Other Words than Love

There are other words besides love we can honor. There is
self-respect (self-love); there is beauty (the recognition of that
which can be loved and cherished in other things and people
and in ourselves); there is control over our lives (for what,
for what?); there is community (of what?); there is passion
and compassion (the capacity in each of us to what?). These
and other words are what we use to describe what we want and
what this society perverts. And they are important words. But
all of them have come to sound a little euphemistic to me. They
are words we use because we are embarrassed to say we want

love — need love — feel broken inside day to day because we are denied love. And so long as they prevent us from saying that, they are bad euphemisms. Because without their roots in our own immediate human ache, they are too distant. Community becomes something enjoyable, a pleasanter way to live, rather than an absolute human necessity. Beauty becomes something that could be spliced together in a good Hollywood film studio. Compassion sours and becomes the distant emotion called pity. Passion becomes an excuse for mutilating the world.

Love and Wholeness

I have said that love is our desire to be whole, to overcome the conflict between ourselves and others, but obviously I have to make my meaning clearer. And I want to do so in a way that shows that what I mean by love is what in fact most people feel when they feel a capacity to love, and not just some philosophical abstraction that is unrelated to experience. Note that I say *feel*, not *think*, because what we think about love is only confusedly related to what we feel. What we think is mixed up with what we have been *taught* to think, which like other things we've been taught is a way of discrediting and repressing the meaning of our experience. To understand what we *feel* we must ask ourselves carefully what is it we have felt when we were in love, and think hard, really hard, about what it was like, what we really carried inside us when we were loving and being loved, what really really happened. If you can answer that question and at the same time have some intuitive sense of trust in your answer, then you can say that you are talking about what it feels like to be in love.

When I try to do this, what I come up with is that one of the things I have felt most strongly when I was in love is an acute, self-conscious sense of myself, a heightened awareness of all my being, a knowledge that was in touch with parts of me that previously I had only vaguely sensed existed, but a self-consciousness that arose not from some fear of what other

people might see when they looked at me, but a self-consciousness from deep within. That is, what I think I have felt is a
sense of my *whole* self. And what is more, I have felt glad with
what I felt. Not because it was beautiful (although it is when I
am in love that I feel more beauty than I feel at any other time)
but because I feel my own raggedness without feeling that I
must turn away from it for fear of being hurt. I am aware not
only of what is beautiful in me, but much that is ugly. The difference is that I am able to look at the ugliness with a matter-of-
factness, a detachment, a recognition that the ugliness is really
a part of an external shell I would gladly discard were it only
safe. And to the extent I am aware of other people, and invariably I am more acutely aware of other people, I am less
afraid to let them see me and less offended if they don't. And
what is more, less afraid to look myself — at them as well as me.

And what I feel of the person I love comes first from my
sense that he is the source of this new feeling inside me. My
sense of her comes from the feeling that here is a person I can
trust knowledge of myself to, who will not use that knowledge
to hurt me (like everyone else has, does). My sense of her is
that I have trusted another person to keep part of myself
inside of her, which is the deepest trust anyone can put in
anyone. But even my statement of it is a little bit nervous,
because the suggestion that you let somebody "keep" part of
you is framed in the language of an old fear — that they might
actually keep part of you, take it away, destroy it and you. The
happier expression of that same feeling, which none of us are
ever quite able to love enough to let happen, is that you and
another person are in some way one, that you share something
of each other in such rapport you are never afraid it will be
taken away. And if you do not fear losing yourself in another
person, if your heightened sense of yourself is so complete and
so strong that you know that person's identity does not
threaten your own and never will, then you feel that you and
another person share of one another in such a way that you

are each other, sharing an essential identity which is the same.

But we are too nervous about love to ever really allow ourselves to become that way. Our sense of ourselves is so permanently incomplete, our earliest love of parents so systematically abused, our sense of self so regularly taken away from us by other people, that the very notion that we should be one with another person is slightly repugnant to most people. We can only think of it as a loss (albeit a loss of our poor, defensive, embattled sense of self).

When I am in love, I usually feel (even though I fail to demonstrate) the capacity to love more than one person. And that is particularly true if it is a "good" love relationship — not one in which I am lost in her or she in me. The tension (conflict, fear) that has been reduced between her and me becomes almost a symbol of how tension could be reduced between me and others. And that capacity is latent and infectious. Other people respond to me differently, are aware of my awareness.

All of these images and many more are images of wholeness and unity. Love is the attempt to be whole. It is the desire to overcome the tension between ourselves and others as the only conceivable route to wholeness. It is the expression of our frustrated oneness with the universe.

But even here, I have talked about love as if it were a personal capacity, and that is because it is almost impossible to talk about my experience of love in any other way. I find myself saying things like "we do not let ourselves," or "too nervous to ever really allow," when what I should say is "we have been too terribly injured, made too neurotically nervous to be able to love." But the deepest part of the social ideology about love is its personalness and privateness, and try as I may, that social ideology keeps reinserting itself in my interpretation of experience. It is almost impossible for me to imagine love as a social experience, as a society. So I keep seeing my failures as personal failures. And the social ideology that makes me see things this way is extremely critical for the maintenance of this society. Because so long as people think of their inability to love as a personal failure, they will continue to believe with part of themselves that love is really an illusion, a romantic, adolescent idea, pretty to look at in the movies, pleasantly painful to remember from your own adolescence, but in the last analysis something to be turned aside cynically, like fantasy and unreality. Like so many other things, the experience of love is turned against itself. We are made to feel that the experience of love is so absurd in this society that it really can't be an experience at all but must obviously be a fantasy.

Love and Technology

The other evening I sat down to watch a movie on television. It was one of those evenings I thought TV was designed for. I wanted escape time to get tired enough to go to bed, hoping I would wake up the next morning refreshed enough to forget my depression and start with a "clean slate." For two hours or so the machine did its job. I sat and stared at it, in some undefined state of mind only remotely associated with consciousness, and watched a movie which less than a week later I have totally forgotten. But this, after all, was what I was looking for, a sort of temporary lobotomy to walk my nervous system till bedtime.

The problem came when, the movie over, I flipped the switch and returned to the country. It was as if I'd turned off some sort of vibrator in my body rather than a picture tube in the room. What I felt was more than the instant re-emergence of conscious depression upon realizing I'd wasted another evening. What I felt was a more decisive, deadening emptiness, a sense that more than time had passed — a sense that shards of content and meaning that had been strewn around in my depression had been washed out of me — a sense of being almost physically diminished. Perhaps I felt this so strongly because it had been a particularly long time since I had looked at a TV, but I realized later than what I felt then I had felt frequently (perhaps always) before when I had spent time watching TV.

Perhaps the reason love becomes such an important, semi-articulable human need at this time is because the external systems we are connected to have become more blatantly alien. Like good Americans we attempt to consume, even attempt to consume in the way we are really supposed to, as a method of deadening ourselves, as a self-conscious addiction to things that will "entertain" us while we sleep our lives away. But it works too well. The consumer is consumed. Over and over again, twenty times a day, we are reminded that it is not we who deign to organize objects and machines for our entertainment, but objects and machines that organize us for theirs.

We turn off the TV; we are empty. We finish with work; we are empty. We shut off the car; we are empty. We finish the Mr. Ice Cream special; we are empty. We smoke the cigarette; we are empty; we smoke another one. We return from the party or the baseball game; we lay down the bridge hand or get off the self-powered mower, or wash off the face cream or the blemish remover; lay down the newspaper, or the news magazine, or the newsletter — or the literary journal for that matter. We are empty. Why?

And if there is no direct answer to that question, there is a consciousness that our material culture has turned on us and there is some recognition, immediate and intuitive, of the gaping hole it has made in us.

Without trying to say that this society is more repressive than earlier societies, it is clear to me that the nature of advanced industrial technology creates more situations in which man sees himself objectified, recognizes the alien objects of his alienated labor coming back to harness him, recognizes himself as the vassal who must serve the needs and carry the ever-increasing weight of a vast, deformed technology.

It may in fact be that earlier civilizations were just as tyrannized, but the heart of the tyranny was more deeply hidden. The web of kinship, the ritual of life that was spun into that web, your sense of the integrity of your family kept you from understanding that the society itself, not some class or interest group, was the core of the tyranny. But now even the last link of that old, soft net of kinship, the nuclear family, seems to be crumbling in the West. Instead of the steady, integrated purpose and certainty even our own clan system gave to Americans fifty years ago, we have an army of objects and objectified relationships *promising* us integrity and purpose but *giving* us instead the daily dose of humiliation and pain and emptiness. And the nuclear family, in its paper houses in the suburbs, collapses under the weight of attempting to rationalize so much shit. Divorce rates go up almost as rapidly as "illegitimacy" rates, the streets become unsafe to walk as the society is buried in a crime wave it professes not to understand, the churches experience a revival which only serves to demonstrate how utterly they have been sacked of any "religious" sense by their bureaucratic and material ascendance, and we suddenly find ourselves thinking that love is the name of the thing we are denied.

What is love? It is a man's recognition that he and his brothers have been objectified. And it is only as Western history begins to rip itself apart on the logic of its own technology that we begin to see that. There is an issue beyond the contradictions of capitalism. The issue is what we gave up for the privilege of being socialized. The issue is simply that the basic learning of all learning is how to override your instincts, and the basic message of all civilization is that the animal must be beaten to death in order to create the man. In order to keep a society alive (*not* its individual members), we must mutilate animals so terribly that they will need speech to articulate their pain and eventually television to wash away the memory of it.

It is that simple; being socialized means being plowed under. And being plowed under means being denied the possibility of love. But plowing people under must be done effectively if the mechanisms of vassalization are to be internalized. Otherwise people become sullen and rebellious, the streets become unsafe to walk, and great amounts of force must be expended to keep people in check, which runs the risk of creating even more opposition than there was before.

What advanced industrial technology has done, what TV is doing, is to destroy the mechanisms of internalization. Repression is becoming more and more externalized. "Making it" becomes suspect. Consciously deadening yourself to the pain becomes more and more acceptable, but despite the proliferation of pain killers, more and more difficult. A tiny crack is created between the increasingly externalized instruments of repression and man's sense of himself. If we had a light to peer into the crack we could discover the roots of our injury. If we had a wedge and a hammer, we could break it open.

The Socialization of Love

What a reactionary upbringing does, what America does in the name of growing us up, is make us the victims of the most elementary shell game, which amazingly enough we fall for. We are told love is a private thing, a thing between two people of their own creation, a spirit that lives within the warmth of a family, a very secret matter that has to do with adult intimacies and embraces. And we are made to feel the close, sheltered, private nature of love's environment.

But as in all shell games, one shell falls and the other is lifted and we are allowed to see the bright, flashy, fashionable — but most of all pervasive — public side of love. It is the love-is-glamour-sex-power-machines-possessions side of love. This is the "civilized" side of love, the side that can and must be paraded before us twenty-four hours a day. But then the shells are moved again and we see that the private side of love is really the civilized part, the dull, domestic, table-mannered, tune-out-other-people's identities side of love. And as the shells

are switched again we see that the public side of love is the
wild, uncivilized, stormy, exotic, orgastic side of love. Here is
where people break loose and live. And the shells keep switch-
ing and our images bend and blend until we don't know what
we are looking at — the public, throbbing fantasy world, or
the dull, unhappy domestic world.

As we try to develop our own private love life, we are
tormented by the public fantasies and the orgastic liberation
they promise. Our sense of love is whipped into a throbbing
desire to look like a cigarette ad or a cowboy movie. In trying
to make the worlds touch, we fantasize the people with us out
of existence, except sooner or later (usually very soon), the
people emerge from behind the fantasy and we experience another disillusionment. We are trapped. The public side of love
is unattainable outside of the movies. The private side seems
more and more to resemble economic cohabitation. All we are
left with is the memory that love once seemed very important
and real. And by the time you are grown up, if everything
goes right, even that memory begins to fade.

Love is Impossible

The fact that this society has constructed us so that we can
never ever let go of enough of our defensiveness to ever really
love someone honestly and deeply, the fact that love is impossible, makes love seem closer to me. The knowledge that I
am not permitted to love relieves me of an enormous sense of
failure and guilt, which in turn has made it much easier to
forgive myself for all the terrible things I have done to other
people, which in turn relieves me of the responsibility of
denying my guilt and blaming my atrocities on another person,
which means that I don't have to be so hostile to other people
and myself, which means I can relax a little bit about me and
other people, which means I can actually open up a little bit,
which means I get closer to love.

Knowing that love is impossible gets me out from under the

thumb of two tyrannies. The first, I call the tyranny of liberation — which stated most simply is the belief that love is possible. In our society, the belief that love is possible is called "youthful idealism." It is an optimism about love that has grown not out of what we have observed in our parents' "love relationships," but out of a feeling for what we have been denied. Particularly when you are young, you know that love is real, because of a constant craving ache you have for it. And since we have grown up in a society that has told us that what is real is possible and what is impossible is unreal, we naturally assume that since love is real it is possible. The connection of our knowledge that love is real to the society's contention that what is real is possible creates an image of liberation. We now believe that we can attain love and the personal liberation it promises. But we can't and we don't; we are far too crippled.

But when we fail to accomplish the possible, when we can't find love, we either blame ourselves for our failure, or we conclude that since love now seems impossible, it must be unreal, an adolescent fantasy. Either way, our belief that love is possible leads to despair and cynicism about love. And either way works out perfectly for the status quo. Because our failure and disillusionment and despair remains focused on ourselves. Our belief that love is possible, our image of liberation, tyrannically forces us to carry the weight of our failure, prevents us from ever identifying the cause of our humiliation.

The tyranny of liberation is believing that the reality of our needs can overcome what this society has done to us. That is not only wrong, it is arrogant. It is one of our most impotent conceits. Regardless of what we say about the power of the military and the corporations, we seem to be incapable of believing that the society that crushed our parents could crush us in the same way. We assume we will do better than them. (We deny that they could ever have been like us.) What we cannot comprehend is that our parents too might have had images of liberation once. We fail to see this because our parents make it almost impossible to see. When their own tyrannical images of liberation crushed them, they lost track of the reality that had been tangled up in those images, they buried their own vivid sense of need when they discovered it was impossible. And better yet, for the purposes of the society, they conspired to deny that there had ever been real need there at all, learned to call it fantasy, learned to insulate themselves from the pain of their loss by pretending that the crumbs of self-respect and the pale reflections of love that the society had allowed them were really quite enough. And although we "see through" the pretense and recognize that much of our parents' lives is sham, we fail, in collaboration with our parents, to ever see the pain that made the pretense necessary. We believe so deeply in our own images of liberation that we walk right into the same trap that our parents did. We pursue love and fail. We blame ourselves for our failure.

But to realize that love is impossible is to begin to work out of that trap. Love *is* real. But love is not possible. To understand that love is impossible but real is to formulate a revolutionary proposition about the society that made love impossible. It is a way to make our vivid knowledge of the reality of love into an anchor that can be used to fight this society. It is a way to begin to make images of liberation that will liberate us, not conquer or tyrannize us.

The second tyranny, which is really the corollary of the tyranny of liberation, is the tyranny of failure. Despite the fact we start out "believing" love is possible, we know that it is not, consciously or intuitively. Our whole lives have been records of failure to find love. Probably the very earliest memory anyone can have in this society is of his failure to keep the love of his parents — of "realizing" one night when you were an infant that your mother had just denied you her love because you'd wakened her once too often. From then on, our lives are records of love getting twisted and denied and used like a whip and just plain lost, so that we know from before we ever start a conscious quest for love that we have failed to find it. And it is natural enough that we would want to guard ourselves against the pain of trying and failing once again. So even as our sense that love is possible, our image of liberation, is propelling us into yet another attempt at love, our knowledge that we have failed to find love is making us be cautious and hold something back (or its corollary, throw everything away). We haul our protection against failure along like a watchdog, always ready to tell us if we've gone a step too far with another person, always fending off overtures from other people that are a wee bit too threatening, always guarding a path of retreat we can use for quick escape. My knowledge of failure and my fear that it will be repeated premeditates and predetermines that my attempt at love will fail. In order to protect myself from more pain, I must so thoroughly hedge my commitment in one way or another* that any "serious" relationship is doomed to starve to death regardless of how much time I put into it. It starves for lack of commitment. It starves because part of me has already planned failure so as to ease the pain. It starves because I am afraid to try to make it work.

But of course the tyranny of liberation, the belief that love is possible, the pretense that characterizes all our love relationships, demands that we deny the reality of our failure, demands that we deny the watchdog is there, demands that we pretend we are really trying to make a love relationship work.

But the knowledge that love is impossible liberates us from the need to deny failure. It makes failure seem matter-of-fact — which it is. Because if love is impossible, it is a matter of fact that we have and will continue to fail to find it. And to the extent we are able to acknowledge and experience the inevitability of failure, we can let go of the pretense that it isn't

---

* The other way of hedging commitment is to hold yourself so thoroughly back as to have it appear that you have thrown yourself away, submerged your identity in another person's. In the name of loving someone else, we give up on the responsibility to portray our experience as vividly as we can; we make the relationship basically dishonest by hiding.

there; and to the extent we can do that, we are enabled to have more honest relationships with people we wish to love; and to the extent we can do that, we get closer to love.

The knowledge that love is impossible makes love seem closer to me.

Love and Politics

There is undeniably a big rift between our notion of politics and our notion of love. Our feeling for the word politics is so radically different from our feeling for the word love that there is little chance we would ever think to connect them — and this is true whether we call our politics "new" or "old." People who say out loud that what they want out of life is love, usually call themselves antipolitical. People who call themselves "political" and particularly people who call themselves "revolutionary political" usually don't talk about love, or sail through the subject with a few slogans.

But if the impossibility of love flows directly from the nature of the society we live in, then people who say they are concerned about love must be interested in politics. There is no way out of it. So it is important to try to understand the origins of the intuitive feeling we have that love and politics exist in two radically different spheres.

If you think about it, it seems obvious that our whole big notion about politics is that politics has to do with controlling the very alien universe we live in. We believe that politics is a fight over who's going to manage the factories and although we "know" this is important, try as we can, we cannot make management of the factories feel like an issue that is very important to us. We can understand it on paper and debate it in a bull session, but we can't feel it very well; control of the factories and other such issues still seems alien. Politics is alien. It is not directly about us. It has not connected our needs to the factory — and I don't believe it can. Our need is not to control factories; it is to make factories unthinkable, to destroy the society in which men spend their lives working and living in various kinds of factories. (Try thinking about a suburb as a middle-class factory, churning out batch after batch of delicate, middle-class mechanisms.) Politics is alien because even its most revolutionary adherents have not been able to draw clear, straight, sharp lines between our need and political goals.

It is odd that this is so, because the first lesson the New Left was supposed to have learned from its first and best teacher, C. Wright Mills, was how to "make the connection between personal troubles and public issues." That was supposed to have been the most basic, rudimentary instruction we got about political education. Our task as radicals was to show people how to make the connection between their own grief and misery and the social structure that produced it. So, for example, we were supposed to have learned that this society makes a man hate himself when he can't find decent work, when the truth of the matter is that for millions there are no jobs and that decent jobs exist for almost no one. But we consistently and stubbornly refuse to apply the same insight to ourselves, to recognize that our own failure to find love is not a personal shortcoming but a condition of life in America. In the first place, we have always acted as if we thought Mills's dictum was to be applied to somebody else, not ourselves. We try to connect somebody else's oppression to that great big old alien framework called politics. But it is only when we try to connect our own need to find love to politics and public issues that we realize how revolutionary Mills's dictum was. To make a solid, binding connection between anyone's deeply felt oppression and politics means everything has got to change. First we must thoroughly explore and rework our whole idea of what love is so that we recognize its social implications. And that is not an understanding that can be sloganized or simplified into an "organizing line."

Second, we simply have to shatter all those old political ideas so that political goals are the most vivid, meaningful goals of our lives. Our whole big sense that politics is about the control of an alien world has to go. Politics has to be thought of as the destruction of the alien world and the construction of a whole new kind of power. Only then can the connection be made.

Love and Dominance

A lot of what makes loving another person hard is the battle that inevitably develops about who is to "dominate" the relationship. The battle over dominance is really a contest over whose experience is going to be validated, whose feelings are going to be recognized as legitimate. For example, I refuse to comprehend the bitterness of a friend of mine. I ignore it by calling it immature and excessive, tell my friend that she should let go of her bitterness like I do, argue that her frequent outbursts of pain hurt *me*, demand that she at least learn self-control enough not to lay her bad trip on me. And when a problem of understanding is posed this way — and so many problems are — it is clear that only one, if either, of us can be understood. Either my friend understands herself as I do (emotionally immature) or she forces me to understand myself as she does (intolerant, unsympathetic), or, what is more likely, neither of us understands either of us and we continue the round of recriminations and build the base of acrimonious tension that seems to underlie so many of the relationships I see and experience. And even if she tries to internalize my judgment about her and keep her bitterness in check, some part of her has been humiliated by my morality. Right at the bottom of our deepest relationships, our competitive identities intrude; we realize that no matter what we want, there is a contest. One person's identity is only maintained and strengthened if another's is forced to yield.

But recently, I have begun to have another feeling. I have begun to realize that the only way to really understand another person is to understand something about yourself. That the only way I can understand my friend's bitterness is to explore my reasons for being hostile to it, and it is only when I explore that hostility that I discover that it is my own bitterness, not hers, that I am hostile to (afraid of), bitterness that has been trapped so far down inside me for so long that I fear it like a man climbing a volcano fears an eruption. I cannot understand my friend's bitterness unless I understand my own. That is why it is so hard to understand other people; it requires that we move onto very treacherous ground. And rather than risk self-recognition, I usually find some pleasant part of my friend that complements some pleasant part of my own exterior, and we share this mutual complement until the unobserved, unattended frictions between us tear us apart and send us hobbling along in search of another victim.

The only way we really have to understand others is to understand ourselves. To the extent that our understanding is detached or distant from us and who we are, it is superficial. Because to completely understand someone else's experience would mean to know the expression of that experience so vividly in your own life that you would share it, and to share it repeatedly would mean to create one common experience where before there were two. To try to understand completely all the experience of another person would mean to create one person where before there were two — and of course we can't afford to risk letting that happen. Because although we are desperately anxious to find someone to share our experience, we are even more desperately afraid that we will get lost trying to understand theirs. We believe we could be tricked. And we believe that because we have been. Always before, in the name of teaching us and loving us, people have tricked us into seeing things their way and ignoring ourselves — us. It is quite simply the fear that we will be tricked again that keeps us from knowing ourselves through other people. And the best way to avoid being tricked is to trick the other person first. So our lives become intricate patterns of deception. We learn to protect ourselves from everybody around us by sealing off or deprecating or dominating the parts of them that feel threatening. And the more effective we are in doing that, the more we are complimented by the world around us for appearing to be "independent," "self-sufficient" people. But of course what we have done in sealing everybody out is seal ourselves off from ourselves. We live in a fiction that tells us we can shut part of other people off from us and be free of the consequences. We pretend that we can watch our brothers dying without dying ourselves.

But imagine for a moment what it would be like if we could throw off all of this defense and counterdefense and really learn from everything we see. Think of what it would be like if we could actually make ourselves grasp and feel what our minds tell us is logically correct — that in comprehending any man's experience, we comprehend ourselves. Believing that would make it possible for us to see the truth in all human experience (including our own), would make it possible to understand that whatever any child sees is real. And imagine what it would be like if we lived in a world in which everyone believed that they could know themselves through the experience of everyone else. The release of locked-up capacity to understand would be quite beyond what we are capable of imagining now.

I do not believe that the capacity to see would be limited to seeing people, because our current defensiveness with other people obviously spills over into a defensiveness toward our entire environment. Think of what we could know in each move of a leaf, each strand of a spider web, each flake of snow, each feeling and fragment of life that goes by every day, unnoticed and untouched, regarded only through the rutted, scarred, regimented prejudice we call consciousness and language.

The Difference between Love and Freedom

I can remember in Atlanta in the fall of 1962, sitting in a tiny office in the black business district, hearing the most powerful music I have ever heard in my life. Pale white, liberal bureaucrat that I was at the time, I was singing too, acutely aware that I was not experientially in tune with the powerful instrument that surrounded me but singing nonetheless, because not singing would have been like being pounded by the waves of a powerful ocean storm and deciding not to swim. And that was long before it had ever occurred to me that drowning might be beautiful. So I sang. And sang for all I was worth.

It was on a hot October afternoon after the first terror-filled summer SNCC had spent in Mississippi, unaided by rich white liberal Northerners and the publicity they brought with them, unaided by anything other than some mystical/political belief that if you could "crack" Mississippi the whole South would come tumbling down, and a determination to turn SNCC into the instrument that would open that fissure. The day before, the summer had broken itself into a thousand pieces in a demonstration in McComb that had resulted in mass arrests and serious beatings and had driven the SNCC staff into retreat in Atlanta to try to pull themselves together and reach back down inside to find the energy and courage to return and continue in the Delta.

I was sitting in the SNCC office as people in twos and threes got back from Mississippi and breathed easily for the first time in months. And as more people came they began to sing, hard and deep, near tears, near ecstasy, as near to emotional unity as I expect a group of people ever gets. And I sang too. As unimportant and as unheeded in that room as any lost man in any vast ocean.

Most of the songs registered themselves in feelings, not in words, but one I remember, and croak to this day when I have the right space and the hope, just sang Freedom over and over again. The song slowly built an image, again not in shapes, but in feelings, that I still retain.

Freedom was a host of people marching down a road, out of the ruins of a lost unhappy civilization that lay as wreckage around their feet. Freedom was well-muscled men glistening wet with sweat, laying sledges on rocks, boasting to the sun that they could work all day without losing a fraction of an instant in their rhythm, without losing a moment of joy in their bodies, because the rocks they were cracking would make the foundations of a new world of Freedom, and because the labor they gave was their own. Freedom was straight, tall, beautiful women holding their naked babies up to the sun. Freedom was the endless noise of little children running from schools after being locked up all day, shouting to release the long pressure that had been building in them, mixing their voices to hear the echoes intertwined. Freedom was a magnificent song that was in all life, that moved with the Master Rhythm and sounded of the chord that first filled the void at the beginning of the universe.

Those images are more than my projections onto the music. They are images that are like the feeling that was in the music, and even if they suffer from all the translations they have gone through to get to this paper, they are nonetheless reflections of what was being said in that room. I know this not only because of how deeply they are marked on me, but because the images, although they do not contradict them, do not mesh completely with my own images of love and liberation.

The separation of men and women, labor and childbearing, is too strong. It is not basically chauvinist. It is simply a matter-of-fact, primal sense of separation, an observation of the beauty of human difference that implies no status and no burden, an image that is only subtly bent if it is men who hold infants to the sun or strong women who toil effortlessly in the heat.

My image of love, as you must sense by now, is different. It is more pastoral, less cathedral. It is more sensual, less sexual. It is more tribal, less civilized. But in the deepest sense, it is part of the same music I heard in Atlanta. It moves to the same Master Rhythm. Its trembling vibration reverberates from the same Master Chord.

6

Love and Sex

Love is not sex. And although this is a statement that we have all heard and "know" at some level, it is a statement that needs some discussion since our experience with love is so intertwined with and so complementary to our experience with sex. But let me say it straight out first and then try to explain.

Sex is a basic animal drive. Love is the organization of that energy into a more human creation that does not throttle the animal, but has as its primary goal the resolution of the conflict between private self and public self, the struggle between me and others. Sex is also a basic animal distinction between male and female. Love is the conjunction and transcendence of that distinction.

Think of what the goal is, sexually defined, of making love to someone; that is, the image we have in our heads of what we would like to have happen. And the answer, if you think about it, should be something like simultaneous orgasm — a *unity* of sexual response that culminates in both people coming at the same moment. That is true, I think, even for people who are deeply involved in male dominance and female submissiveness. The man wants the woman to give herself to him completely at the pinnacle of his conquest, to melt satiated under a hot flood of sperm. Nothing less will assure him of his ultimate potence and her complete submission. And she in turn must be involved in hoping for complete destruction, to be obliterated in her responsiveness to him so that she becomes him, opens herself so completely to his motion that she dies in his climactic explosion.

Bad images as I think these are, I think even they can be used to show that love is not sex. For in our collective fantasy world where such conquest and such submission is realized, simultaneous orgasm is followed by *peace* and *deep sleep*, the complete relaxation of sexual tension. The reward that the motion picture stud gets for screwing another incredible blond is a momentary respite from his constant state of hyper-masculine tension. And in our own fantasies about such perversions, the reward we get is a respite from never-ending anxiety about sex, and in that moment when all tension is released, we are able to feel as one with one another, no longer crippled by our crippled sexuality. In our imagery about successful sex, the desire exists, just below the surface, to bring an end to sexual tension.

But there is a question that should come up about the example I have just used. Isn't it just as possible (and a good deal more honest) for a man not to look for orgastic unity and peace, but to achieve his masculinity by causing the woman he fucks extraordinary pain, by subjecting her to pure, passionate, sexual brutality? And for that matter, isn't it more consistent for the woman to be involved in that kind of sadomasochistic joy than in the relationship described above? The answer in both cases, I think, should be yes. What is called a sadomasochistic perversion of sex is really, if you think about it, the logical way for sex to take place in this society. The logic of social attitudes toward women which sees them as sexual objects, inferior to men, created to serve man's need, should be expressed in sexual intercourse. The logic that sees men as voyeurs, consumers of sexual objectification, masters of sulky, sensual creatures who crave domination, should also occur in sexual intercourse, and that does not happen if sexual tension is released, but only if it is aggravated. And that cannot happen with simultaneous orgasm, a release of sexual tension. That can only happen if the man is totally satiated and the woman is totally brutalized, if his ego is completely fulfilled and hers completely humiliated.

In fact, it is probably true that most people actually participate to a degree in this symbolic expression of our literal social relationships. Almost all men want to hurt "their" women. Almost all women, at some level, have been successfully trained to call their pain joy.

But to me, the significant thing, considering the nature of the society that we live in, is not that there is such a widespread participation in sadistic symbolism. The significant thing is that there is almost universal resistance to that symbolism, that when we embrace each other in bed, we so literally embrace the contradiction between portraying our socially defined roles (sadomasochism) and our desire to escape them (love), and that the goal for most people, consciously or not, is not to succeed sadistically but to find sexual unity. Underneath their attempt to portray their sexual roles, people are looking for a

way out of them. People are looking for love. People are looking for peace and a deep, untrammeled sleep in the arms of
another person.

Let me rephrase what I originally said. When I say that love
is not sex, I mean explicitly that insofar as love and sex are
connected, love implies overcoming sexual conflict and corro-
sive sexual tension. Love is the conjunction and transcendence
of sexual distinctions. And if you think about it, that applies
just as obviously to the possibility of love existing between
two or more men or two or more women, as it does to love
existing between men and women. It is worth mentioning, but
hardly needs elaboration, that the sexual tension and constraint
that exists among men is enormous and makes a veil of fear
that erodes the possibility of love. And it is just as clear that
the negative, competitive identification women have toward
one another is also deeply limiting.

And what all this points to is that our sexuality, like so many
other things, has been inverted, used against us, used by the
society to lock us up in lonely places no one ever finds. We
have all been perverted, and consciously or intuitively, we all
know that to be true. If we are to understand what our sexuality has to do with the capacity to love, it will be found
not by looking for the answer in the erotic fantasies where we
have been taught to look, but in trying to discover the roots
of our perversion.

It is the fact of sexual repression that registers most emphatically, if not first, when we are young. By sexual repression
I mean a general physical deprivation. Our society detaches us
from our senses, our physical sense of ourselves, perverts our
natural physical capacity to feel and touch and see and taste
and makes it irrelevant or counterproductive. The social pressures are so much stronger than the physical drives that the
physical becomes folded and compressed and knotted inside a
process of social compaction.

The city, for me, is the symbol of that physical contortion. When I come back to the country after even a moderately short time in the city, I must literally recycle my senses. It takes me a week to begin to smell again. At first there is the strong conglomerate smell of the country, of earth and leaves. But gradually that breaks down into a much subtler sense of a thousand things. I can smell the time of day, the kind of day, the wetness in the air, the dryness in the leaves, the way the ground will feel when I walk on it. My senses get reconnected; I begin to breathe differently, farther back in my lungs, deeper, so that my nose works. When I'm in the city, I do the opposite; I almost consciously begin to mute my senses, breathe more through my mouth, in the top of my lungs, to keep out the air and the smell, pull my senses in as close as possible, though even then they are drenched and overridden. In the country I am aware of my capacity to listen to things that are close to me or to listen to things that are far away. In the city I am hardly aware of my capacity to listen at all. In the city I am almost never really hungry for food (it is the equivalent of always being compulsively hungry); I eat irregularly and mechanically, I eat bad food that is quick to fix or get and easy to swallow without an appetite. In the country, I begin to crave food, eat better even though I have to cook everything for myself, gain weight, and amaze all my friends who concocted such good things to try to get me to eat in the city. And more than any of those things is a pervasive sense of being a more natural man, of being in touch with myself, of knowing the awkwardness and agility of my limbs not through their observation by others but through their *physical* (but now we need a better word) connection with a physical self.

In part, this is the wrong way to present what I want to say, because it sounds as if I am contrasting the natural beauties of pastoral living to the destruction of human capacity caused by urban life. It is not so simple in my mind and I should make that clear. Because for me, the country is a somewhat contrived respite, not from *urban* constraint but from *social* constraint. It is what the city represents socially much more than its physical perversity that shuts people off. At some point the physical and social reality of the city become synonymous, caricatures of each other, but it is the social congestion, not the physical congestion, that deadens one. Indeed, the country I talk about is, once you begin to know it, remarkably congested with life and cycles of change. But one can know and relate to the congestion of the country without losing touch with oneself. That is almost impossible in the city or in this society. Only in a totally different society can I think of being really involved in a congested social reality in a manner that did not destroy my senses.

In some ways, I think our other physical deprivations are even more ominous and complete than our sexual deprivation. At least we are aware of sex as a problem, but most people are so out of touch with their bodies that their physical alienation only infrequently causes anxiety. As a result, all of the repressed physical energy gets focused on a desire for sexual liberation which short-circuits our sexuality, overloads it with too much of a burden, makes us wanton, and in the end contributes substantially to our sexual frustration. It is only the reconstruction of our physical senses as a whole, a consciousness of their integration (integrity) that is worth calling liberation. Sex is the exposed, sensitive member that the society caresses and tantalizes until we are dominated by sexual inducements and fantasies, but we could not be played with so brutally if our physical understanding of ourselves was not so fragmented. Our physical repression is general; but the alarming thing is that, outside of sex, it is so nearly complete.

Another way of saying this is that social constraint, the destruction of love in social relationships, is the instrument of deprivation of our physical selves. We are out of touch with our physical selves in order to be in touch with the society around us, the society which has taught us that it is the giver of life and meaning. So the society gives us sexual roles to perform, which, if you think about it, are more than sexual definitions, but are fairly comprehensive physical descriptions. They tell us how we are to walk, how our clothes are to fit (tight, loose), how we are to look at our bodies, or hold things, or touch and look at people.

But sex is the theme our attention remains focused on, or maybe I should say our anxiety, because it is such anxious attention. From at least the time of adolescence, we are conciously and almost constantly aware of our sexual inadequacies. Our anxiety does not arise primarily out of the fact that children are frustrated at an early age from attaining a primary object of sexual desire (Oedipal complex). We are quite capable of dealing with some sharp frustrations without turning ourselves into neurotics. But we are perverted by a society that trained our parents to lop off our senses in order to make us reliably neurotic (always hungry).

But I should try to be more concrete. Part of our personal quest for love is a quest for sexual liberation or at least good sexual relationships. People, in the remarkably tight ways we talk about sex, will acknowledge some of the pure adolescent anguish they still feel in an awkward sexual encounter.

To deal with our anxiety, a progressive subculture of sexual educators and counselors has grown up. They have discovered that sex is an art (not quite a science), and even have books from ancient China and quotes from respected Greeks to prove it. It is understandable that we might be a little bit anxious about sex, say these progressives; who wouldn't, it being such a complicated matter. This statement is followed by several libraries of material which in most spectacular detail show what a complicated art it is.

These progressive sex philosophers tell us that although a good sex relationship is not the only source of a happy marriage (most of the books skirt the problems that come from other kinds of relationships), it is a necessary ingredient. And

although we might chuckle at the triteness of such profundities, they register. Because you know what bad sex has done
to relationships (or you will). And maybe you know how important good sex was to a good relationship before it went
stale. And the worst thing is not bad sex but mediocre sex, because then you don't quite want to admit that you're bored
or unfulfilled for fear of hurting someone you care for or
being hurt yourself when the accusation is flung back. And in
that situation, who can know. Is it me? Is it my failure, my
lack of potence? Does she really want me? Why don't we
make love as often as we used to? Could she be seeing someone else? Is that the reason? No — impossible. I know her
better than that. Perhaps I should look around.

But the sex philosophers have a way out of it all. If it is bad,
it can get better. If it is good, it can be kept from getting
boring. Lovemaking is, we discover, not some innate capacity
of manliness or feminineness, strength or beauty. It is an art.
And you can be an artisan. Everyone, even someone with a
very small penis and no past luck, can learn the art. And that of
course is a tremendous relief. Because we are never allowed
to forget our sexual inadequacies. We must constantly com-
pare ourselves to the public sex-fantasy people and at each
comparison find ourselves inadequate and wanting. And most
of us are so wanting.

So we read the books, buy the props, even begin to talk
about our hang-ups with sex, and try technique twenty-two A.
And in fact, we do amazingly well. Given the amount of pressure there is in this country to perform sexually and how high
the stakes are, it is amazing that most young people can even
fart when they first get into bed. The fact that eventually
almost everybody does have sex suggests that the social pressure to have it is stronger than the socially induced fear that
you might fail at it. And probably the books help, although
I suspect that their real contribution is in assuring us that we
can make it and not in all those groovy new positions.

But the real problem with the books, whether in the short run they "help" or not, is that they carry with them a social ideology that is as much a part of this society as the war in Vietnam or poverty or racism. Their real effect is to alienate people further from their sexual capacity and to substitute a technical understanding of sex. Sex begins to be understood as a set of positions, proper manipulation of "erogenous zones," foreplay and afterplay. We are technical men in a technical society and we must have technical sex. To say that sex is natural and that everybody is born knowing how to make love not only would not sell books, but wouldn't be believed by *us*. True, there is some logic to the notion; animals seem to get on with a minimum of study. But the books inform us that our social taboo about animal sex, which we find ugly or repulsive or embarrassing or just plain animal (an interesting derisive term in our culture), is a well-founded taboo. Man improves on nature. He substitutes for the hot, smelly rut of animal love the sophisticated subtlety of the art of erotica. But the real reason we can't believe it is because if we thought sex was natural (and naturally beautiful) there would be no explanation for our anxiety and our sense of inadequacy. Except, of course, the real explanation, which is that our natural capacity has been so decisively plowed under by the society that we must imitate mechanical man in order to accomplish some sexual satisfaction.

But the real explanation is hard to come by. Maybe because if we could answer honestly what we most feel about sex when we are young, the answer would be fear. The fear is not artificial. It may have been unnecessarily and artificially induced, but the fear is quite real. It is the feeling you almost have to have about your sexuality, growing up in this country. If there was some way we could listen to the fear, even acknowledge it to someone we cared about, it might be a powerful guide back into ourselves. But the society has things to say about fear too. Fear is to be overcome, in the sense of put

down, conquered, vanquished. Fear is a sign of cowardice,
inadequacy and impotence. It should never be allowed to direct
us. "The only thing we have to fear is fear itself." Fear is
childish. And perhaps the fear we fear most is the fear of sex.
For a man to admit to a woman that he is afraid of sex is almost unthinkable (and for many men, it is quite literally unthinkable). And it is only a slightly less dangerous emotion
for her. (Although to the extent that there is a difference,
women seem more able than men to talk among themselves with
some honesty about their sexual experience.) So we are locked
up with our fear. And our fear is locked up in us as a hated
emotion, constantly being pushed back and denied.

Among animals, fear is a sensitive instinct, a guide to self-
preservation, the instinctual capacity, reinforced by experience,
that leads the animal to heightened awareness of its surroundings and the possible dangers in them. It seems to me that one
of the most astonishing accomplishments of civilization is the
creation in men of a social fear of their own instinct for self-
preservation. Fear of fear. Distrust of our own sense of danger.
Denial of the emotion that is telling us that we are about to
injure ourselves, destroy ourselves. Damage to the capacity
that tells us that we are about to be damaged. Only in such
a world could we have the situation where the beginning of
sex becomes for many, perhaps for most, the beginning of a
more or less psychologically destructive experience.

But you will want to know why I think that fear could guide
us back into ourselves. Because we have been told that fear is
a "blind" emotion. It is supposed to cloud our other emotions,
make us incapable of "reasoned" (try substituting conditioned)
responses to danger or adversity. But your own experience
should tell you more. When you last got frightened when you
were alone in a house, contrary to blinding you, your fear
gave you new eyes. You could hear everything: every creak
of every old board, every rustle of leaves or twigs outside.
You could hear so much that you couldn't be sure that what

you heard was really as it should be, whether you were actually alone, or whether the house required the help of someone else to make all those noises. (Incidentally, had there actually been someone else in the house, your chances of actually having heard them would have been much better. The only question is whether your fear of fear would have prevented you from acting on what you heard.) What blinds us, if anything, is a fear of fear; a denial of it, an unfamiliarity with it; a refusal to accept it as natural and proper and listen to it, to take cognizance of our surroundings and try to find out what is wrong. The emotion in a deer that brings his nose to the wind, his ears erect and his body ready for flight, is not wrong if nineteen out of twenty times he discovers nothing wrong and returns to grazing. The twentieth time (or the two thousandth) it saves his life. The other nineteen times it reassured him that the world was as it should be and helped to heighten his capacity to detect changes in his environment.

All of this is to suggest that to listen to the fear we had (have) about sex would be to listen to the feeling that something is profoundly wrong and dangerous and to look for the source of danger. And there is a faith in me (it is other things, but it is most simply that) that if people were able to acknowledge their fear and listen to it, it would tell them that what they were afraid of was the absurd, awkward, mechanical consciousness the society had given them about lovemaking. They would understand that what the society wants people to do in bed is basically dishonest; they would begin to lose interest in acting out a social sex role, of posturing before someone they cared about, particularly insofar as that role requires the denial and masking of fear. They might even begin to believe in their own sexuality and understand that it was not something that was given to them on the condition of performing a role (fulfilling a stereotype), but was something they had always had.

I am not saying that there is some innate, desirable, animal state of sex that we should return to. What I understand to be the essence of our humanity makes that impossible: our reflective consciousness about ourselves and our actions is not shared by animals. But I am saying that to cut man off from his natural, animal sense of himself, makes him a neurotic, sensually depraved creature whose social conditioning negates his animal capacity, makes him constantly at war with himself, and prevents him from ever finding satisfaction.

We have the capacity to direct our senses, to sharpen and refine what they tell us. It makes sense to say that people can use sex to communicate complicated emotions and feelings. That is one of the reasons it is sad we have such trouble feeling sexually open with many people. But that kind of communication can only happen if people are in touch with their sexuality — their sexual sense. To the extent that they have lost touch, sex is directed by external images, which are propped up and kept running by the fact that people are so deeply alienated from themselves.

What we have come to call sexual liberation is a capacity to stagger through our sexual roles with enough outward finesse and technical proficiency so that sexual stereotypes and tensions do not completely demolish our capacity to love — that is, to have some inkling of the sense of wholeness and unity with and through another person. At times, some of us (and perhaps with the aid of the progressive sex subculture, in time, most of us) come to feel moments of sexual transcendence. Or perhaps I should say transcendence of the received social ideology about sex. For it is at those moments that sexual categories and definitions melt, and some innate sexual sensual capacity reaches up and finds itself in another person.

One last note. One of the recollections I have of sexual play (note the words we use) in the days before I ever made love to a woman is that the best times were extended erotic encounters with a girl that were not really that frustrating because they did not culminate in intercourse. Not that there were no special pains reserved for that period in my life. But most of those pains had to do with the kind of masculine exploitation I was mandated to undertake by my peers. "Did you feel her up? Did you get her bra off? How many handfuls has she got? Did you get in her pants? Did she get in yours? Did you make her?" And I believe that girls had their counterpart to my mandate, which was to tease, "keep him interested," but "not let him get too far."

My recollection is that I did not much like the obligation of seeing how far I could get, perhaps because I feared that I would get too far and actually find myself having to have intercourse with a girl (a fear, of course, I never admitted, never could afford to admit until years later when I had had "successful sex"). But conscious fear that had much more to do with my easy embarrassment, shyness, and most of all my fear that my sexual overtures would be rejected or found clumsy and repulsive. But there were times, with some girls, when there was some understanding about the "limits" of our sexual play and when we liked each other well enough not to be always consciously bent on exploitation and manipulation, that I experienced a kind of erotic joy that is really quite different from intercourse. And the difference, understood in retrospect, was that in my adolescent sexual encounters, I knew that there would be no release of sexual tension, other than perhaps a very gradual waning of interest in the erotic play. But in adult sexual encounters, my erotic attention is focused on orgasm, on its release, on my release from it.

Adult sexual liberation requires that we destroy sexual tension, largely, as I have suggested, because the sexual categories we operate from are so oppressive, and the tension they create so damaging to our capacity to love. The books, of course, say that unrequited sexual tension is all wrong, physiologically and emotionally. And I remember a period when I used to think back on adolescent sexual play with compassionate condescension for the poor young me who was cut off from "full sexual expression." But I wonder now. I wonder whether, if we lived in a world where sexual objectification and categorization had been destroyed, we wouldn't be released from the social mandate for orgastic sex (equally the adolescent mandate for non-orgastic sex). Try to think what our sexuality would be like if it was really ours, to use and direct as we pleased. And if you can find images of that, then I think you will have begun to find images that describe the connection between sex and love.

Part 2

Class and Separatism

7

Separatism

What I have talked about so far in this book can be fairly concisely summarized. I have been trying to illustrate, with a variety of metaphors, one simple thing — that even though human nature, which I call a capacity to love, has been defiled, our experience still gives us an intuitive recognition that we have been oppressed.

But recognizing we are oppressed is only the beginning. That knowledge, in and of itself, doesn't point out a direction to move. The way most of us experience oppression is as an amorphous, omnipresent sense that is so diffuse we cannot locate its source or articulate any of our feelings about it. On the few occasions when we do strike out against it, we strike out blindly and impotently, blow up or "lose control," and of course feel childish and ashamed of ourselves afterwards, whether or not we are forced to admit it by way of apologizing to the people we "offended." Alternatively, we build great, rationalistic constructs to describe Oppression, which may sound quite articulate, but do not connect to us.

What we need is more than the knowledge that we feel oppressed. What we need is a way to sharply define oppression and disentangle ourselves from it. Properly understood, the process of defining oppression is not a process of abstraction; we are not simply looking for a set of diagrams or generalizations we can make about the society. Our first task is to make concrete, not abstract. Our first task is to bring back, validate, make more vivid, our own authentic experience. We need to get in touch with our own pain and joy and try to remember what caused them. That is a funny kind of abstraction; it is abstraction that takes place only when we have recalled all the details we were told to forget, only when we have gotten further into the particulars of our own experience than we have ever gone before.

Stated another way, what this society makes us feel is a deep inauthenticity about ourselves. Even our outbursts of rage seem wrong — inappropriate and immature. What we are looking for is authentic identity, a description of ourselves that we trust intuitively. And the only way to grasp that new identity is to sort ourselves out from "them," to reverse the process that has led us to internalize our own oppression. I call this process of sorting out separatism — quite literally to separate yourself from your allegiance to the system that oppresses you. And it is that process I want to talk about in this chapter. In addition, I want to talk about the fact that large groups of people share the experience of oppression in such similar ways (share the same basic political metaphors) that they can separate themselves (search for authentic experience and identity) collectively. I call such real or potential collectives, classes; I call the shared metaphors of experience they have, class experience. Basically, what I want to do in this section is sharpen, refine and politicize what I have said so far.

Let me begin by going back to the alley and the boy and the rat.

All of us experience a disjunction between personal experience and social experience. The disjunction is frequently painful — that is, we are punished in some way for holding out our interpretation of experience against the correct social interpretation. The punishment may not be quite as literal as being spanked for saying there is a rat in the alley, but it is real. We have all met people for whom the disjunction seems to have almost completely disappeared; indeed, it is hard to imagine that it ever existed. We cannot imagine what they were like as children; they seem always to have been old — exactly as they are. These are the people whose identities have become so merged with the jobs they have and the social life they are supposed to lead that one has the feeling that there is no residue of resistance. The archetype in our society is the corporate man — perhaps the forty-year-old Madison Avenue ad man on the make who is an utter creature of his condition — an utterly conditioned creature. I am not particularly interested in him — other than to examine him as an adversary. But I am terribly interested in the kid who saw the rat in the alley and what he felt when he got spanked for reporting what he saw. Certainly part of what he felt must have been shame and just plain hurt for having led his mother to withdraw her love from him, and just as certainly, he must have felt that he must avoid displeasing her so again. But another part of him must also have felt resentment, sensed the injustice of the spanking, because after all he did see something in the alley.

That resentment and anger are the psychological and political beginnings of separatism — and separatism is a fundamental ingredient of revolution. Had the kid responded to the spanking by telling his mother that he still knew he had seen a rat in the alley and that he always would and that nothing she or anybody else could say or do would ever make him stop seeing rats in the alley, he would have in fact separated himself from her and what her authority represented in a critical way. We would immediately recognize him, even as a child, as a "rebel" and a "fighter," although we might also acknowledge, as we are supposed to, that this child has an emotional problem — what else are we to say about someone who sees rats when we don't?

But we also know how unlikely it is for a child to actually take — not to mention maintain — this stance. In a very literal sense, his parents are too powerful. They not only have physical power over him, they have the power to deny him their love — and although that is a weapon he can reciprocate with, it is really too terrible to contemplate. He is too isolated. The punishment even further isolates him. In the end, the resentment, along with the emotional vividness, is likely to get plowed under. But social revolutions are precisely about people seeing things in the alley their oppressors don't. It is precisely people saying there is injustice in the alley and on the streets and in the shops when their oppressors say the streets and shops are filled with justice and progress even if there is an occasional mugging in the alley. It is people saying they see no recourse when their oppressors say there is recourse. But, most importantly it is people saying this who have heretofore been part of the oppressive system, who are emotionally and experientially tied to it, who have been taught all their lives that it is always right and they are always wrong. The emotional magnitude of separatism, whether it comes when you are a child or as part of an adult movement, is enormous. Think of what it means for a Chinese peasant who has grown up under a land system that is thousands of years old and whose justification permeates every aspect of life, religion and philosophy to say that that system is totally unjust and must be overthrown. Think of what it means for a Negro who has spent all his life wanting to be white, wanting to have what white men have, to suddenly say, I am black and beautiful and no longer part of your goddamned country. Think of what it means for a woman whose identity has been so shaped around learning how to be pleasing, submissive and subservient to men to suddenly say that she will no longer be sexy and coy and alluring. Those moves are gigantic. They are done in the face of enormous sanctions which are all the more frightening because in the past they were so deeply internalized. And they are doubly hard to make by yourself. If there is no one else who sees the injustice that you see and you persist in seeing it, you are likely to wind up, in this country, as a discounted eccentric or a certified lunatic. But if your recognition triggers (or is triggered by) recognition in other people, there is a greater chance that you will not be discounted or locked up (at least not in an insane asylum), and by the same token, a greater chance that you will not wind up repudiating what you have seen with your own eyes. It is for this reason that we must be interested in class, because almost no one believes deeply enough in what he sees to persist in seeing it when everyone else insists there is nothing there. We need allies. We need people to stand behind us when we finally stand up and say, "Mama, you're dead wrong; there *is* a great big ole rat in the alley, and *you* are going to have to deal with him."

I am not saying here that what I call class oppression is necessarily our deepest oppression. I believe we are all most deeply oppressed as human beings (that we all share the same essential oppression) not as blacks or women or proletarians or Algerians or Chinese peasants — but as human creatures. But between us and the possibility of relating to one another directly as human beings — quite literally and deliberately preventing us — lies an enormous cultural, political, economic residue called class experience. That residue does not totally prevent me from having some sympathy for, or even empathy with, the plight of a woman in this society or even, through the medium of a book like *Fanshen,* the plight of a Chinese peasant. But all the sympathy and empathy in the world does not change the fact that I am still tightly sealed in my own cultural envelope, I must still strain empathy through the restriction placed on me by my own oppression. Until I make my own break in my own name, the deepest emotion I can have for a Chinese is essentially charity and self-pity, noblesse and despair. What I am saying is that I believe that the deepest form of experience we have that is coherent (intelligible, capable of being grappled with) is class experience. The deepest, clearest political metaphors we have are class metaphors.

Like so many other points in this book, the final argument for this point is intuitive. Either it feels right to you or it doesn't. Many I think will feel that their class experience is so pervasive as to be invisible (incoherent) and therefore unavailable for any kind of reflection or action. But even if you do feel some intuitive agreement with my formulation, there is still the question, what is my class experience, what is my class? Because in case you haven't noticed, I've defined class rather circularly, subjectively and conveniently as the deepest coherent, collective experience you can identify. For example, is a black woman in this society oppressed most deeply as a black or a woman or is she forced to describe a unique category of oppression called "black women," and if she describes that category as relevant, does that prevent her from working with black men or with other women at this time? All I can say about all of those questions is that I do not believe they are questions that I or other intellectuals can answer out of some theoretical schema about how things should *be.* They are questions that black women must answer out of their own intuitive insight into how things *are.*

Meantime I have enough troubles of my own. Is middle-class really the relevant category of my class experience? My answer, as revealed in the next chapter, is yes and no. Yes, insofar as it is a relevant, coherent set of experiences that I sense we must define and repudiate — separate ourselves from. No, in that it still feels intuitively not precise enough. There is some subdefinition of middle-class (try intellectual or man or upper) I am looking for that will resolve the ambiguity I feel. Or perhaps not. Perhaps it just takes a little bit more time till it all sinks in about what it really means to allow yourself to be middle-class in this society. I do not know the answer to that question, but I do know that the instruction I'm looking for is intuitive, not academic.

Separatism is not exactly a path you follow by choice. All of us are too committed to our humiliation to do that. We love our chains. They are what have made us "secure" all our lives. The security may have been impacted with enormous misery, but it has been presented as the only way to live. Part of our indoctrination is to make all other ways of living seem impossible or degrading. I suspect we give up our security only when we're "forced" to, only in the desperate situation where the only way of life we've known no longer seems capable of sustaining us. Maybe that suggests why revolutions seem so frequently to take place when situations are changing "for the better." It is not just that things are better; it is that the old way of life has crumbled; there is no way to hang onto it; there is nothing to do but propel yourself out of it. (The old way crumbles in America.)

But even when the old way clearly won't work anymore, you don't turn to separatism. First you try integration. You try to make yourself fit into the life you don't fit into, but it is impossible. The United States tried to fit into Britain. Algeria tried to fit into France. Black America tried to fit into white America. Women tried to fit into male society. But it didn't work. They just didn't fit. It was not logically impossible. It was empirically impossible — it was experientially impossible — it was intuitively impossible. And when there is no place else to go, the result is separatism. You can't go back (to the old way). You can't go forward (to integration or reintegration). So you are forced to go your own way.

But the same conditions that create the necessity of separatism make separatism absurd. It is almost always so. It is absurd on the face of it. How could the Moslem population of Algeria expect to run their country after a hundred years of extensive French colonization and acculturation? The Moslem population was poor, malnourished, and technically illiterate. It could never expect to run the complicated society that had grown up there. It would collapse without France. Clearly, argued the French, the only possible reasonable course was integration. But the Algerians said integration was impossible. Separatism was the only way. It was absurd.

Or look at the absurdity of black separatism. How can black people even dream of separating themselves from America? They have been part of it for three hundred and fifty years. Where would they go? Back to Africa! If blacks persist on a revolutionary course they will be obliterated. But blacks say it is the only way.

And finally there is the absurd beyond the absurd — women's separatism. What do they propose — a society without men! It's impossible. Men are necessary. Whites are necessary. France is necessary. Mother is necessary. We the oppressors are necessary. You will die without us. We will kill you if you try to leave us. Anything else is absurd.

But the separatists say it is the only way. You have tried throughout our history together to integrate (read: dominate) us and you have failed. Now we will do the impossible. We will build a new, autonomous life for ourselves out of ourselves.

But you will still insist that it is absurd. Blacks and women

are radically different examples from Algerians. Algeria was
an external colony, not an integral part of America like black
people and women. And colonial revolutions are as old as the
American revolution. Be that as it may, what I want to stress
is that to the average Frenchman, and certainly the French
cologne in Algeria, the proclamation in 1954 by the National
Liberation Front that Algeria would be independent must have
seemed equally as absurd as does the prospect of black people
separating from the United States. Technically (logically, empirically) it is not that much more difficult. What is important
is not the technical difficulty but our (the oppressors') attachment to it. It is clear that this country will kill thousands,
perhaps millions of black people, before they force us to do
what is technically fairly simple. Our attachment to our racism
is that deep.

Again, it is not the technical difficulty but the emotional
inconceivability that prevents us from considering women's
separatism. After all, it's a rather simple matter to kill male
babies. Only a handful are necessary to propagate the species.
As a matter of fact, with modern methods of detecting the
sex of unborn children improving all the time, it would be
possible to abort male pregnancies quite early. It's even reasonable to expect that with some research a way could be found
to separate male sperm from female sperm so that only females
would be conceived. (Thus even Catholics could participate.)
And while we are being reasonable, it is reasonable for women
who have been oppressed through sex and by sex all their lives
to consider that the simple, obvious, and perhaps the only
solution to their oppression is the removal of the oppressor.
It is even worth thinking for a moment what a unisexual utopia
would be like. (If your immediate response to that suggestion
was to chortle something to yourself like "a lot less interesting," or "not nearly as much fun," then you should be good
enough to admit to yourself that you are not in fact emotion-

ally up to thinking about it.) I am not advocating it. I am merely saying it is contemplatable, and the contemplation need not lead to an image of something terrible.

Separatism is absurd. There is no doubt about that. But its absurdity has much more to do with the intensity of the injustice that spawned it than with the technical or logical absurdity of the separatist proposition. The absurdity we sense about black separatism and women's separatism has to do with the fact that they occupy a kind of revolutionary frontier in our country. We "understand" colonial revolutions and peasant uprisings only because they are remote and historically behind us. For the oppressors for whom they represent the present, separatism still seems totally absurd. To try to be human and free in this world, no matter where you are or when you are, is obviously absurd.

But all of this only implicitly speaks to why separatism is necessary. Let me try to be more precise. The necessity of separatism grows out of the complete moral ambiguity that precedes it. The child learns to hate himself for seeing what his parents can't see. That is to say, our oppression is so deep and is internalized so early that we eventually lose track of where it came from and assume we are to blame. There are, of course, ways to straighten yourself out; every culture provides them. You can, for instance, take out your anger for your parents on your little brother, or you can become a "success," but that does not get you to the source of your anger. You can even take out your anger at your parents on your parents without getting to the source of it; it's quite simple; you simply do to them what they did to you — deny the validity of what they see and experience, refuse to acknowledge that it is real. Naturally enough, in this situation you hate yourself for hating your parents — love-hate-self-hate. The way out of that dead end is more than the repudiation of your morally ambiguous family experience. The way out is a moral affirmation of your real experience. It is a black man *remembering* that he is beautiful and simultaneously re-pudiating the culture that told him he was ugly and it was beautiful. It is a little boy remembering he can see and simul-taneously repudiating the culture that told him he couldn't. Separatism is inextricably linked to the way we learned our current feeling of who we are. We learned by forgetting. When we remember what we forgot, we must simultaneously remember what made us forget it, and repudiate it. Those two things, taken together, describe the necessity of separatism.

8

We Are Not Middle-Class

*or We Not Only Need
a Name for the System,
We Need a Name for Ourselves*

In 1965 I got a lot of attention in the small world that was then the student movement for saying at the SDS march on Washington that we had to "name the system" that made the war in Vietnam and the countless injustices of American life possible. A few months later, Carl Oglesby gave another speech to another march on Washington and picked up where I had left off. He gave the system a name — corporate liberalism — in a speech that described with remarkable effectiveness the rationalistic dehumanization the liberal credo apologized for in corporate America. Later yet, people began to feel more comfortable in calling the system imperialism or corporate capitalism or just capitalism. Recently, a friend of mine remarked at a meeting how far we had come from the name-the-system speech in 1965, since we were now unembarrassed to say what we all knew then — that the system is capitalism and the movement is about the destruction of capitalism. The meeting was one of those unhappy sectarian quarrels, so I didn't feel free to say that capitalism was not the name I was looking for in 1965 and was not the name I was happy with now — nor for that matter was corporate capitalism, or imperialism or Oglesby's corporate liberalism — though if I had my choice, I'd take Oglesby's before the others.

What I meant to say in 1965, and what I think Oglesby meant to say as well, was that we needed a name to describe what was wrong with America that had authentic political content for us. I did not fail to call the system capitalism because I was a coward or an opportunist. I refused to call it capitalism because capitalism was for me and my generation an inadequate description of the evils of America — a hollow, dead word tied to the thirties and a movement that had used it freely but apparently without comprehending it.

I talked about the system not because I was afraid of the term capitalism but because I wanted ambiguity, because I sensed there was something new afoot in the world that we were part of that made the rejection of the old terminology part of the new hope for radical change in America. I was disappointed in Oglesby's speech not because I disagreed with it (I thought it was brilliant), but because it sacrificed the ambiguity which I felt was such an important part of our movement for a term — corporate liberalism — that didn't particularly stir me.

The importance of all of this is felt more clearly in retrospect because there are some things I understand now I don't think I did then. The first is that the singular, authentic identity of our movement was (is) the most precious thing we had (have). It was and is our chance to develop a radical middle-class movement into something much more powerful. The name we are looking for is a name that not only "names the system" but gives us a name as well.

Just as blacks had to say: "We are not Negro. That is their name for us. We are black men. The system is not segregation; it is racism; it is white oppression. Our movement is a black power movement for black liberation."

Just as the Algerian nationalists had to say: "We are not French. That is the name they give to those of us who they have totally destroyed. We are Algerians and we always have been. The name of the system is not discrimination; it is colonialism. Our movement is a national liberation movement. Algeria for the Algerians. We are the national liberation front of Algeria."

Just as women have had to say: "We will no longer be 'their women.' That is the name they have given us. It means 'out of man.' The name of the system is not discrimination against women. It is male oppression. It is the oppressiveness of so-called male values. We are a women's liberation movement, but we will give ourselves our own name. Henceforth we are witches."

So too we must begin by saying, "We are not middle-class." Our first task is to reject the definition the society has given to us. It is a critical step in finding not only a name for the system, but a name for ourselves. What I want to begin to explore in this chapter is what it means for us to separate ourselves from middle-class identity.

We may have been born middle-class. Our parents may have struggled all their lives to make it into the middle class and give us middle-classness. But we are not. We are off that trajectory. Not out of its grip; like the slave who gains emancipation is not out of the grip of the slave system; but out of touch — ideologically.

There are some people who talk about the awakening of the middle class and who urge us not to forsake our heritage but to realize that the sixties betokened a revivification of the American middle class, an awakening of its conscience and energy, a sudden awareness of itself as potentially powerful in moving the country toward more humane and enlightened civilization. Projects such as Vietnam Summer (1967) were partially conceived with the idea that it would be possible to send alienated youth back into the suburbs where they would find for the first time receptivity to their political concerns, and presumably a respite to their sense of isolation from their roots. And that is no doubt true. Increasingly, the people who build and live in the suburbs are afraid of the bomb, want an end to the cold war and the most obtrusive forms of social injustice, want the air and the cities cleaned up, bigger parks, more theater, a smaller oil depletion allowance, and even, I'm sure, a more reasonable attitude toward drugs. And these are our demands, are they not? ("And they'll raise their hands sayin', 'We'll meet all your demands,' and we'll shout from the bow, 'Your days are numbered!' ") They are our demands if you think of demands as the (broken) fragments of a social image that could conceivably be acted upon by a legislature in this country. But they are demands without their essence, vitality or spiritual meaning. They are the reduction (inversion) of an image into components that add up to less than the sum of its parts, that add up to the old society, spruced up a little here, toned down a little there, but basically the same. And that is what the people who build and live in the suburbs are committed to. They have a deep ideological stake in that society; it has paid them well for their allegiance, and although they may want it greened up a little ("This summer we're going to fight the crabgrass"), they want it. We don't. We are committed to its antithesis. That is why we must begin to separate ourselves from the middle class. What we are about is not its revivification but its destruction.

Making concrete what I call an antithesis (separatism) can be done in a variety of ways. I want to start with what I think is most visceral — what the middle class "stands for" and what we stand for. That is important to me because I can remember a time, not so long ago, when I felt that it was important to affirm certain aspects of my middle-class heritage, to acknowledge that many of the values of the middle class were my own. Now when I reflect on those values, I am amazed at how superficial my understanding of them was, or more likely, how hard I was trying to be generous and inclusive in my definition of who "we" were.

Let me begin where it is simplest. *The middle-class image of the good society is at its root competitive.* It is an image of men struggling against men, whether in athletics or international trade or the new gray-flannel ad/business man — the nicest house, the finest car, the best taste, the most beautiful children — the erudition of the professor as he puts down an upstart student, the quick jibe, the biting sarcasm, the finesse of the modernist political candidate as he parries newsmen's questions with wit and factualism under the glare of hot lights and the pressure of high stakes. Even where the society admires collaborative efforts, "teamwork," it is always adjunct to competition, as again with athletics or business, or the space-race teamwork of NASA, the Huntley/Brinkley team beating out the old-style CBS news coverage, the teamwork of the tactical police crushing a street demonstration before it could become a riot.

The middle class feeds on constant grading and evaluation, the never-ending social intelligence game that gets formal glorification in schools, chicken-judging contests (I was champion Champaign County chicken-judger when I was twelve), the office, the art festival/contest, popular music ("And now,

Number One"), classical music ("And now, see whether you recognize this all-time favorite"). But more insidiously, and perhaps more important, if you're young, at a dance or in a swimming suit or driving a car or making small talk, or even when you finally make the team, you're still getting judged, graded, classified, ranked on a hundred competitive scales, by a thousand competitive eyes.

Our image is at root collaborative. It is an image of a society where men's estimates of themselves or each other are not developed out of a contest where one man wins and another loses — where one is one up and the other is down.

Today's middle-class world establishes itself on the notion that social and personal space is scarce, the idea that you've got to fight to get as much as you can and protect it from all those (and they are almost everybody) who are out to get it. The suburban home is the most graphic visualization of that; it struggles to appear open and green, broad and expansive — big — but the man with the lawnmower, moving up and down in his yard, harbors the fantasy of himself as a sentry, guarding the small world that he has spent his life acquiring against all the multitudes of enemies who would take it away from him. Despite its size, it can never be secure.

It is perhaps out of our own sense that space *is* scarce, that the world that we live in is congested, that we have come to the conclusion that it must be shared. The way to create more space is not to knock down the man in front of you or the tree or the mountain or the people or the nation, but to find a way for your sense of yourself not to be dependent on taking someone else's away. It is a much more complicated image than the old one, but it is also a much more deeply felt need. Basically, it is the need for love. We do not want to live in a society founded on competition. We thirst for communalism — a capacity to share (not hoard). We are tired of looking over our shoulder to see what people think, to wonder what they are putting in the record. We are tired of calibrating life and computerizing character. We have no desire to be president of General Motors *or* the University of California or first on the moon or last to break in the push-up drill. It is more important that five people sit quietly in a room listening to music that they all are moved by than that the Beatles be number one. It is more important that one man ski down a mountain alone with the spectacle, beauty and freedom of that motion inside himself (not contingent on his costume or his appearance in other's eyes) than that Jean-Claude Killy be world champion skier.

The middle class is committed to progress. It equates progress with technological prowess and the sheer volume of the material load that our civilization can move around in the course of a year. The middle class is involved in the image that the struggle and sacrifice is to bring about progress and it identifies with the statistics that "prove" our advance — bigger buildings, faster planes, electronic wonders like computers and cybernetic factories, super superhighways. People who stand in the way of progress, like railroad firemen or the old building trade unions, the Sioux Indians or the latest victims of the thruway project, are in varying degrees pitied and despised — but uniformly judged wrong through a powerful, objective morality that finds them guilty of impeding, being in the way of, blocking, retarding, hindering progress. But note that the "modifiers" are all partial or have partial connotations. For progress is never stopped; it goes on throughout history, removing impediments like a glacier removes boulders — slowly but irresistibly. Life itself is progress — progress in learning to walk and talk, progress in toilet training, progress through school and college, making progress with a woman or a firm.

If there is some consternation in the face of the undisguisable destruction that results from unleashed technology, there is an abiding faith in the capacity of the same technology to correct its mistakes. If the air and the water were polluted by certain kinds of machines, then other kinds can be invented that will fix it all back up. If the Appalachian economy was destroyed by strip mining, automation and the progress of the oil and gas interests, then some federal highways and modern job training techniques will bring tourism and light industry to "restore" the economy. If the Sioux Indians have their homelands buried under a flood-control project, then progress, once again, as it has so many times before, will move them and their entire little civilization to higher ground, and compensate them well for the inconvenience. If people develop cardiovascular disease at thirty-five because they no longer use their limbs and exercise their circulatory systems, then surely medical science (which is so astounding) will soon provide new drugs and plastic hearts and veins to "cure" or replace the old (we could hardly say worn-out) system. Indeed, "We have the technical know-how to do all these things now, if people are willing to pay the price." And increasingly, the middle class shouts back, "Pay the price; pay the price."

Even the bomb, which did as much as anything to alert the middle class to its precariousness and to its conscience, turns out to be the exception that proves the rule. (Read with a deep, grave voice.) "Thermonuclear energy provides man with his greatest challenge. It could either be the instrument of his destruction or, if harnessed, the creator of unlimited energy."

"Pay the price; pay the price."

Progress in the end, it will be conceded, is difficult, complex, even risky — but worth it. And to be completely honest, it will be conceded that certain inevitable dislocations of people and resources (shall we call them culture lags?) accompany even the most orderly technological progress. In fact, only a few men at any one time could ever be assumed to be abreast of this rapidly changing age. But the rest of civilization has kept pace remarkably well, don't you think? In the end, man always shows himself to be adaptable to progress; he is a remarkably resilient creature.

Progress is our enemy. Of all the bloody altars that man has erected throughout history to sacrifice himself on, it is the bloodiest.

The notion of progress starts with the extraordinary assertion that technological development and human development can be equated. It is an article of faith. The short and simple of the meaning of progress is that men must be mated to machines, made to function like them, at their pace and with their kind of minds. And women must learn to clasp the resulting cold steel between their legs and call it a man.

Progress must be stopped. It has nothing to do with people or their needs. It is the thin philosophical apology for letting machines control civilization.

The middle class stands for expertise. It makes sense, since that is what the middle class is all about. It is composed of the people with the technical and social skills that are required to run the progress machine, and it is sufficiently self-impressed and specialized to have created a cult of itself, a cult of the expert. Let me illustrate with a TV ad by a New England bank, which is trying to sell people on the idea of a "personal investment counselor." The ad shows the man sitting in the middle of a circle of empty folding chairs, in a rather bleak, darkly lit room. As the announcer reads off the categories of the man's personal counselors, the room fills up (and brightens up) with a doctor, lawyer, clergyman, insurance man — everything you need except, of course, a personal investment counselor, who soon enters the room brightening everything to its peak and relieving our anxiety. All the counselors would look identical to anyone reared outside of Western civilization, but our well-trained eyes can instantly pick up the deliberate distinctions added to the TV stereotypes — the somewhat more somber look of the minister; the older, reassuringly mature feeling about the doctor; the harder, pinstripier edge to the lawyer; the affable, nondescript quality of the insurance man. Everything is perfect, except the man in the middle should be a quadruple amputee. It is clear that that is what we are meant to feel he would be without these trusty servants.

This society has not only created a dependence on experts, but has rationalized our insecurity about the control they have over our lives into a cult of the expert. You may not have the faintest idea what the physician is doing to you, so to compensate for the anxiety that creates, you choose to believe in him — and if not him, then medical science. There are intuitively well-known hierarchies of experts (with the physician very near the top), but they all represent, more or less, the amputation of important life functions from our control and understanding. It is worth noting that working-class experts fall near the bottom of the hierarchy — for example, the mechanic, who is so intimately involved in our egos since he works on our cars, is almost universally distrusted. There is no more reason to distrust him than a doctor; in fact generally, I suspect that mechanics have a relatively more thorough knowledge of their field than doctors do of theirs and are at least as honest. But the mechanic is distrusted, largely, I suspect, because he lacks the pedigree — quite literally the breeding, manner and qualities of middle-class social skill that would put us at ease. The need for pedigree, then, becomes an essential part of education, at least as important as the technical knowledge the expert masters. And that need is increasing. The more specialized and fragmented the society becomes, the more need there is to keep it glued together with extensive and careful "pedigrization." The top engineering schools, for example, now cram more and more liberal arts down the throats of their students; it is not just vogue; it is a critical effort to hold the society together.

The kind of glue I'm talking about is the kind we've all been

trained to disbelieve the reality of; it is *ideological;* it is a faith
in the essential soundness and coherence of an incomprehensible
system that is ratified by the fact that the system emerges
triumphant everywhere we look. It is not a faith that can be
simply subscribed to by proclamation. One must be initiated
into it over a long period of time. One of the reasons the middle class was so horrified by Lyndon Johnson was because of
his Texas vulgarity. He was a professional politician of the old
style. What was wanted was a man of middle-class sensibilities,
a man with the style and manner of an expert who could
reassure the middle class that "our kind of guy" was at the
controls. Kennedy, who was our kind of guy, was forgiven
the Bay of Pigs and the Cuban Missile Crisis — acts so brash
that had Lyndon Johnson committed them, they would have
aroused a stream of unending horror and "shocked indignation."

What the middle class wants is not so much a set of political
acts, but a style of political craftsmanship that assures it that
a bearer of the faith, an expert, progress-oriented leader, is at
the controls of our technically complicated civilization.

We stand for the destruction of the cult of the expert. Perhaps the simplest assertion the New Left has made is that people have the capacity to make *all* the judgments about the
critical things that affect their lives. If a man is so estranged
from his body that he has nothing to do but place it limply
in the hands of a doctor, then he is philosophically, physically
and emotionally in bad health, regardless of what the doctor
does for him. If a man's ego is so deeply involved in a machine
that he is completely incapacitated when the machine breaks
down, his need is not for a trustworthy expert to fix the machine but for a new relationship with the machine or no
machine at all. If civilization is too complicated for ordinary
men to direct, then civilization is at fault and not the people.
If we must have Shakespeare experts in order to "understand

and appreciate" Shakespeare, it just may be that we can get along without Shakespeare. Expertise is the bond of faith, the ideological glue that covers up our mutilation. We would be whole.

The middle class stands for security through possessions. The accumulation of property and wealth is the most significant measure of that possessiveness. But the most dynamic characteristic of possession and security is the acquisition of status. The possession of status, power and stature, the quest to be somebody big, someone people know about, someone who is feared more than he fears, someone who moves in exclusive circles, who has prestige — that is the real drive of middle-class possessiveness. What people are looking to possess is a *position* above other people — in a sense, the possession of other people as subservient.

We are not involved in your quest for possessions, human or material. You have given us no model of integrity in human relationships, but we know that is what we want. So long as one man's security is another's insecurity, we will be content to share our insecurity. Your property is boring; there is too much of it; it is tasteless and heavy; it sits there, for the most part unwanted and unused. It dominates your lives; you must constantly protect it, refurbish it, insure it, paint it, mow it, shingle it, display it and attend to it emotionally when it chips, splits or cracks. When your children go away from you, your devotion to it becomes pathetic.

But at this point, I have to admit that what I have done so far in this chapter is a little bit unfair. Because in a fairly heavy-handed way, I've stressed a description of what the middle class *is* rather than what middle-class people might like to be. And no group is particularly happy in being talked about simply as it is; all of us want our aspirations acknowledged as real, even if they are remote. All of us need to have our good intentions weighed against the reality that has corrupted them. Most of our parents were at least a little embarrassed by the vacuous materialism they reared us in. If they fed on and helped to create the cult of the expert and personal possession, it was still within a framework of consciously wanting something more for us, even as they became resigned to the notion that whatever it was, it was not for them.

Stated most positively, the social and political aspirations of the American middle class are for the completion of the American revolution — the creation of a society of equality, liberty, and the inviolable integrity of the individual — and from that social vision, which was projected so strongly onto us, came our first sense of hypocrisy and injustice, our first commitment to set things right. The civil rights movement, dominated initially by "middle-class" blacks, began with that vision. The anti-anticommunism that stood ground against McCarthyism came from that vision. The struggle against the reactionary (inequitable) organization of power in the university and other parts of the society began with that vision. And the first clear, moral objection to the war in Vietnam (that it violated the *rights* of the Vietnamese people to make their own history) came from that vision. At the least, we are historically in its debt for having forced us into some sort of confrontation with the world around us, and for many, it still describes the moral conclusion of the revolution they would make. And equally important, it is the drift of the movement away from any clear connection to these moral roots that has made it incomprehensible and alarming to millions of Americans who once thought they supported it.

Liberty, equality, individual rights: these things too are what the middle class is about, no matter how rhetorically. You will want to know whether, in my insistence on inverting my social heritage, I believe we should reject these ideas too. The answer is yes. I do. Let me try to explain why.

To begin with, let me say that all of these ideas are closely, circularly and integrally connected. They form the nexus of an integrated social philosophy. *Liberty* is defined as the *equal* opportunity of all men to exercise their *individual* rights. If it is defined any other way, one man's *liberty* becomes another's tyranny. *Equality* means that no man's *liberty* (*individual rights*) will exceed another's; that all men will have an *equal* chance. The integrity of the *individual*, the cornerstone of the trilogy, is based on the assertion that all men share an essential (*equal*) humanity, which can only be realized if it is protected against all elitist (*anti-libertarian, anti-equalitarian*) ideas. In short, the ideas are really only definable in terms of one another; they form a unified proposition about man and society; they constitute essentially one idea.

The radical or revolutionary quality of that idea is not in question. Even when it is weighed against its corollary idea — that governments are constituted among men to assure these liberties and therefore, by implication, to constrain them where necessary — it still seems self-evident to me that a society that balanced the tension between social constraint and individual liberty so as to maximize liberty would be at least a revolution away from the world we live in now. I think the slogan "participatory democracy," as first enunciated by the New Left, envisaged that revolution. Participatory democracy is essentially radical equalitarianism.

All of this is basic American civics, which regardless of its twisted presentation at home and in the schools, came through pretty powerfully for many of us. I summarize it here so as to point more clearly to the place where I get off.

The questions I want to ask are: what is the central idea of man and society behind equality, liberty and the integrity of the individual? What is the basic social conception they all grow out of? What is the historical force that makes them still seem valid and cogent to so many of us? What is the utopia in which they would all be realized?

My answers to those questions, most simply stated, are that the idea of man behind liberty, equality and individualism is one of an isolated social atom, autonomous and alone; the idea of society is of a mechanism that insures the continuation of such atomization by destroying any force that threatens it; the historical force that ideas of equality and individualism grow out of is not the American revolution, but the industrial revolution which effectively shattered our very ability to imagine society and provided instead an image of anonymous associations of autonomous parts called "individuals." When I think about the utopia in which we would at last all be equally liberated and individual, at best it looks like a watery pluralism in which all social identity must be centrally monitored to prevent any subgroup (whether it is General Motors or SDS) from becoming a threat to the narrow equilibrium in which personal liberty is "maximized."

What does it mean to maintain the integrity of the individual? It means blocking out the possibility of any deep, significant, unifying social structure, because such structures always imply a loss of individuality. For example, the extended agrarian or immigrant/ghetto family of fifty years ago, crippled and dying as it was, connotes to us a loss of identity. We think of our grandparents, and to a lesser extent our parents, as having been fettered by the responsibilities of kinship — tied to parents, obliged to help their family out, even when it damaged their own individual opportunities to grow. And while the conservatives weep and moan for a bygone era and blame it all on FDR and social security, most of us chuckle in our sophisticated college way and say that's the price you have to pay for liberating the individual. We become modern men almost directly in proportion to our ability to feel tyrannized by the very thought of any close-knit human social organization. We are so threatened by the possibility that our individuality might be compromised that we find it impossible to make a workable and significant commitment to any other human being. Our real divorce rate (as measured in attempts to have significant contact with another human being that are eventually broken off) is astronomical. If only the conservatives knew they were the last, most authentic gasp of a group in the society that yearns consciously for its primitive, communistic origins.

Except I do believe that some of us too, who call ourselves rebels, have begun to feel that the thing called individualism isn't all that it's cracked up to be, even if as we feel it, our commitment to the rhetoric of individualism makes us insist there is no conflict between communalism and individualism. Except there is. And we all know there is. If we think deeply about it, we know that any serious attempt to understand or connect to another person means giving up some of the rough edges we call our personalities. It has to happen. There just isn't any other way.

Individualism, as we know it now, began with industrialism and the need of industrialism to drastically remake the social order to conform with its need for interchangeable parts. The logic of industrial individualism demands equality, because the individualist ethos at its root is of a world in which it's every man for himself. And if you know you've got to go it completely alone, that puts a very high premium on being assured you have just as good a chance as the next guy. Individualism needs equality or it erases its contention that individualism means anything.

Maybe that's why the working class has historically been less individualistic. The reality that your individualism is a joke is beaten more ruthlessly into a worker's head by the machine he labors under all day. But regardless of who you are, the myth of equality breathes real life into individualism. Even the factory worker, if he believes in equality, is involved in the search for a fulfilling, isolated life — either for himself or his children. Which explains why the middle class projects equality so vividly into the future and onto its children. Equality is what was supposed to make it all make sense.

My image of equality is a situation where in each generation a whole great mob of us get up at the starting line and start running pell-mell at the future, stumbling and tripping over one another, pushing and shoving, as it is only fair to do, fighting it out until we all get to the end and another generation lines up at the start — except — under equality — nobody gets a head start. And liberty is what an individual is supposed to feel about his life when it goes like that. In the middle of the great race, a man is supposed to stop, breathe a deep sigh of relief, and say "Boy, this is living," peck his wife on the cheek and set off immediately to jump the next set of hurdles. That is what liberty, equality and the integrity of the individual are really all about.

We are not a bunch of disconnected social atoms. We are intricately, beautifully molecular. We are tied to each other so damned dramatically that if the right one of us fails one afternoon when a flock of geese fly over the radar screen, we will all die. We are so molecular that the thoughts of one man pressed between two red covers can change the lives of a billion people. We cannot reduce society to atoms. It doesn't work. It doesn't account for anything important that we know to be true. Life is molecular. We are terribly, objectively, knitted together.

But we refuse to share a common identity, and here, of course, is where our individualism makes sense. It is simply impossible to share a common identity with Richard Nixon. Society has been so organized as to reduce molecular identity to some nationalist or globalist cult. We are allowed to "identify with" Richard Nixon or the moon loon by watching them on television making faces at one another through a decontamination chamber, but that is far too vacuous and remote to have anything to do with common identity.

We do in fact share a common identity, which is far and away the most crucial determinant of everything we are, but we are prevented from experiencing that identity because the society we live in is so antihuman. Only machines could experience the molecular structure of our society — because it is an imitation of them. I want a society that is made in our image.

And in that kind of society, it is hard to make sense of the notion of equality. To say that people share equally in a common identity is immediately to cut it back up into little slices, where everybody gets his own atomized share. But it cannot be like that. At some point, the result of people being able to experience their molecular identity must be cumulative; the fact that people are able to experience their connectedness must change decisively what it feels like to be an individual. It is not that each of you shares a piece of one identity. It is rather that you have one identity which you can no longer think of in pieces.

Furthermore, if people do have some singular, individual identity beyond social identity, I doubt that it is equatable. For example, the difference between me and a tree is irreducible. There is no really satisfactory way to equate me to a tree (or even a bean pole, as so many have tried to do). When it is all said and done, we are quite different and unequatable. But I can understand the way I am *related* to the tree and trees. I can understand the nature of the ecological systems that bind us together — in short, understand the way we are part of one thing — the way we are one. And if I understand that, I am much less likely to lay waste a forest, even though I am irritated that the tree is so arrogant as to be different from me.

I do not need equality. I need unity. And unity, as we've all been told so many times, is one of those fascist/communist words (except in times of national emergency) that is used to steal away our individualism. Precisely. And while the critics cluck "There lies the fascist/Stalinist pitfall, just like we said it was," I will say that is the pitfall we must risk. The other pit is the one we're in, and it is not good.

I would like to be able to think of a man in the way I'd like to be able to think of a tree. It is the only way I can imagine that we could ever come to a situation where we would not lay waste to one another — even though we might, in some ways, be different. I am not talking about tolerance (another great middle-class value), because tolerance snaps the moment anything central appears to be threatened. I am talking about a shared identity that is so deep that even frightening differences can be risked.

I know these are scary ideas for many people. They are still somewhat frightening to me. They smack, not of finding identity, but of losing it. That is because part of our most basic conditioning is to resist any threat to our individualism, and no merely intellectual process can seriously change that conditioning. In fact, what many of us consciously perceived as the need that dislocated us from the society was a need to be more competent, complete *individuals*. We entered the movement or the dropout culture looking for individual identity which we felt we could not get in the mainstream culture. A bunch of words won't float away that need — although it might help to begin to redefine it. Nonetheless, at some level we will remain committed to our individualism; it is necessary for survival. But I do think it is possible to see and even feel somewhat the way in which the perfection of that individualism is not what we want. We do not want to be complete, autonomous men — not quite. Part of us wants to need, and openly acknowledge the depth of the need, for other people.

The other problem with these ideas is that they are much too abstract. What is the kind of society I'm talking about like;

how can I imagine this molecular experience if I'm as stunted as I say I am? And I must admit I can't imagine it very well. But I do have a couple of images of what a society that had shed its atomization would be like. For example, no one would have a highway built through his neighborhood (assuming that there was someone interested in building highways) unless he wanted it. But no one would think of not wanting it if the society needed it. The correlative of that would be that the society would not think it needed it unless it really needed it. A difference of opinion between one man and the community over whether a highway was needed would be a clear sign to everyone that things had to be worked out very carefully. And before somebody suggests that I am slipping individual liberty back in through the back door, I am not. One man opposing the highway when everyone else in the community wants it is not liberty; it is the most solemn obligation. It is not an ego trip. It is an incredible self-abasement before the wisdom of social unity. It is done because you realize that when you cannot understand your connection to something everyone else in the community can understand his connection to, it means that not only you, but the society, is out of whack.

It's like a baby crying and everyone who hears knowing why. And it's like people hearing each other hear the baby and knowing they all know why he cries.

We are not middle-class. But if we are not middle-class, what are we? What is the new name and the new identity we will take for ourselves? What is the name of the system that oppresses us? Is the name that important, is it really? And if you think about it, the answer is yes, it obviously is.

But it is just as obvious that we have not yet reached the point where we can give ourselves a name. It is not possible now. And it may not be possible for a long time. We have got to let go of a lot more than we have so far before we can think clearly enough to come up with a new name. And in part I think it is the frustration of people failing to find that new identity that makes them rally to their sense that they are traitors to what they believe in, and consequently succumb again to the notion that the revolutionary impulse comes from some other group — to the conviction they are illegitimate.

If I was forced to give the system a name now, I would not call it capitalism. I would perhaps say that it was hate and we are love. That it is unattended fear, and we are the courage to attend it. That it is isolation and we are community. I would not call it capitalism because the abolition of private ownership and production for profit is not enough. It does not promise, as Marx thought it would, to create a free and communalistic society. That is a problem beyond capital, beyond the question of whether the equipment that manufactures the material wealth of a civilization is "privately controlled" or "socially controlled." I would not call it capitalism because we suffer as much from the logic of a technologically constructed civilization as we do from capitalism itself. What we experience is depersonalization through bureaucracy, standardization of human beings to meet bureaucratic and technological demands, the destruction of the family and the primary community, the impossibility of love — and all of those things are rooted in a deeper essence than is described by the term capitalism.

We are not middle-class. We are love; we are courage; we are community. They are hate, fear and isolation. That is the beginning of a better understanding.

9

We Are Not Working-Class

To say we are not middle-class implies something not only about ourselves but, if you think about it, about other groups as well. It is traditional for middle-class radicals to admire and extol the virtues of some other class. That of course is because we have been led to understand that a) the bourgeoisie is counterrevolutionary; b) we are the bourgeoisie and therefore counterrevolutionary; c) some other group must be found to make the revolution, which despite our counterrevolutionary tendencies, we may be able to identify with and help along. Never mind that the last clause seems to contradict the rest of the syllogism. (Either we are counterrevolutionary or we are not.)

The main task of middle-class radicals seems to be to develop some symbiotic relationship with the revolutionary class, presumably the workers.

It is easy of course to convince us that we are middle-class. It is objectively demonstrable; it is what we've been told we were all our lives; it is an indelible label on our speech and all our other mannerisms; there is no reason to doubt it. And it is also easy to demonstrate that the middle class is counter-revolutionary. It is also unnecessary since we know it intuitively, but just to reinforce our intuitive understanding, it can be pointed out that the middle class is the most successfully and deeply integrated part of America. It may have some problems, but its essential revolution was won two hundred years ago.

It is also equally easy to demonstrate that other groups in the society have more severe grievances than the middle class. The contradictions of the society rest on their shoulders, and it is their historic task to play out those contradictions through revolutionary action.

Finally, we can easily be shown how the society works on those underclasses (traditionally called the proletariat) like a grinder, honing them against their own exploitation, slowly, generation after generation sharpening their anger until eventually a spark kindles the final conflagration and the proletariat rises up and crushes its oppressors. That is to say, there are *objective* forces working that create revolutionary consciousness. Those same objective forces are presumably working on the middle class, instructing it that at some point, regardless of superficial grievances, its interests are with the ruling class.

There is a kind of easy plausibility to this line of argument that is hard to go against. Not only does it appeal to our own sense of inadequacy, our own daily experience of betraying what we most believe in, but it describes a reality that in part we know to be true. For example, the ghetto uprisings seem such clear markers of the potential for revolutionary violence that is created out of generations of abuse. They represent a potential you could feel in Watts, or Newark or Hough long before it ever erupted. It is hardly a potential you can feel in Larchmont or Park Forest.

But what all this overlooks is that the black or working-class youth is really faced with much the same dilemma that a middle-class youth faces. He is not born into some objectively defined revolutionary subset of America. He may be perceived that way by intellectual revolutionists, but his experience is, like ours, one of being subjected systematically to an ideology that teaches him to deny the validity of his own experience and perceptions and accept the dominant working-class social ideology as the description of what is real and desirable.

Accepting that ideology is hardly a conscious choice. It is part of life — it is a way of life — it is the thought force that has most control over the conflict and tension in your life if your father wears a blue collar. There are some aspects of that received ideology that may help a working-class youth to grow up with fewer illusions about what this country is all about. For example, he is much more likely to inherit from his parents a general cynicism about politics and power and understand that the country is not governed in his interests. But any such gift is two edged. His cynicism about the possibility of access to political power, whether it is in government or the unions, fosters a kind of fatalism about his condition and allows him eventually to be the reliable supporter of the political machines and bosses that look out for his "interests" in the most narrow and limiting sense. Nor does that cynicism protect him from becoming an ardent nationalist and patriot, his country's most reliable cannon fodder. If anything, his political cynicism insures his patriotism as the only available means of national identification.

I do not want to suggest that what I call the "working-class social ideology" is monolithic, no more than I meant to suggest that the received, middle-class ideology is monolithic. There are obvious variations within the broad contours that define such an ideology, and those variations may even be significant in predicting who will first break out of that tradition. Thus for example, some working-class families are intent on boot-strapping, acquiring all the accouterments and niceties of middle-class life and, above all, educating their children to move out of the working class. Others are more "stable," raise children whose expectation is that they will live in homes and work in factories much as their parents did. And just to compound differences, the home that has middle-class aspirations for itself may have inculcated its children with the notion that it is just to struggle against the bosses, whereas the "stable" working-class family may have taught the value that you should get by with the boss and stay away from trouble-makers. But underscoring those differences are the similarities that created them — for example, the belief that manual labor is inferior to other forms of work and that unskilled labor is the lowest form of all. The stable working-class family deals with that belief fatalistically, whereas the family with aspirations "struggles" against it, but both are under its heel and effectively within its grasp.

Of course the fact that any social ideology presents itself in many forms makes its repudiation more difficult because it leads people to believe that there is no coherent class definition of their lives; it contributes to the good old individualist sense that your life is a discreet biography. The question is whether or not people assume that their experience and oppression are shared. And it is important for intellectual revolutionists to understand that a worker can look up from his bench and see a whole assembly line of men who, like him, are chained to machines, and still not have a feeling of shared class identity. Because if at some point the man next to you sucks the boss's ass so he can make it in the factory and eventually out of the factory, it destroys the possibility for a class-based movement. It is not that you see him as a traitor to his class; it is rather that he, and the other twenty variations up and down the line, destroy the very sense that you are a class. They shatter the image of coherent repression. All you are left with is personal rebellion. The best you can hope for is a gang.*

By the same token, what I am talking about explains why revolutionary separatist movements first turn their political fire on their own community and not on the oppressing class. Because the most immediate threat to the existence of their movement is the element within their own community that undermines the newly discovered sense that they are a class. Thus early in the Algerian revolution, the National Liberation Front outlawed prostitution, gambling and drugs within the Moslem community. ("We are Moslems; henceforth we will demonstrate the self-respect that the debased *cologne* culture has denied us.") Or similarly, the Black Panther Party debates whether it can outlaw crimes of violence by black men against black men. The thrust of those efforts is to make people understand that they are a coherent group with a shared identity and destiny and that therefore toleration of exploitation within the community is tolerance of self-destruction.

What I'm saying is that regardless of where (what class or strata) you grow up, the society spawns a pervasive social ideology which presents itself as the primary interpreter of experience. It is not that this ideology has no relationship to objective conditions; rather it grows out of the necessity (human and cultural) for finding an explanation (way of making coherent, rational, explicable, predictable) for why life is as it is. To talk as Marxists have about the revolutionary, prole-

---

* One of the things this makes clear is that the definition of class itself, at least from the point of view of the revolutionary, has an important subjective element. It does very little good for us to see that millions of workers labor under deep oppression, if none of them sees it. We may be able to describe what leads a class to begin to see itself as a class, but my sense is that such description is always *post hoc* and that the opposite reaction could almost always be explained with the same set of information. In the end, it is the change itself (the objective occurrence of the subjective event) that is most important.

tarian values that grow out of the objective conditions of working-class life, is, at best, somewhat confusing. Because to the extent that those revolutionary working-class values grow, it is out of a rejection of other working-class values that people have been steeped in all their lives. If a middle-class youth must say "I am not middle-class" in order to break his ideological fetters, so must a working-class youth say "I am not working-class," or perhaps what he must say is "I *am* working-class," since so much of the received working-class ideology has to do with escaping into the middle class. A revolutionary working class must find an authentic name for itself and the system that oppresses it as surely as we must find one for ourselves. On this score, it seems clear to me that to the extent that middle-class radicals have historically influenced working-class movements in this country (and I think they have mightily), the process of ideological, revolutionary self-definition has been stifled. Because middle-class radicals have been right there with the labels. "You are The Workers, and your enemy is The Bosses." But those definitions are not sufficient. They have failed to create a revolutionary working-class tradition in this country, and accurate as they may be on one level, they are obviously inadequate. The process we are looking for has to do with people comprehending a definition of themselves and their oppression out of their experience. It has nothing to do with pasting hundred-year-old labels onto still superficially explored anger. The sorting-out process is much more difficult.

In many ways, what I have written in this section strikes me as wooden and jargonistic. It seems to be the only way we know to talk about the working class. The problem is that I cannot empathetically create the language to describe what it feels like to be a working-class youth in this country — or any other kind of youth than the kind I am. The emotional/intellectual task of defining his oppression and his rejection of it is beyond my experience. As a result, my attempt to outline "the problem" pushes me back into sociological/political jargon that is as stiff and uncomfortable, as strained by real social distance, as are the actual human contacts that occur between middle-class and working-class people.

But the reason I haul all this dead weight out into public is because of the sense of insight that comes from understanding that I do share with an American working-class youth a similar human dilemma. We were both born into classes that presented themselves as flexible, amorphous, even nonexistent, although their social ideologies defined, shaped and objectified us. In order for each of us to break into his own most vivid reality, we must each be involved in the repudiation of past experience — and the repudiation must be as thorough for him as it is for me. Just as I must understand the link between middle-class liberalism and my oppression and repudiate it, he must understand the link between trade unions and his oppression and repudiate them. And beyond the repudiation, or perhaps out of it, lies the other need — the need for new definition, the need to find a name for ourselves that is our own, a need to find a name for them that they will never be able to deny.

It is true that the circumstances of our birth are radically different and that they surround us with our own peculiar labyrinths. And it may be true as well that my working-class counterpart has a better chance (is forced more unrelentingly by his circumstances) than I to search for an authentic revolutionary ideology (although it has not been proved). And it may be true that having chosen a revolutionary path, he is less able than I to rebuild his bridges back into the old society (although it has not been proved). And it may even be that in the decisive moment he will be better equipped than I to act decisively (although it has not been proved).

But even if those differences are acknowledged, they do not destroy the community of condition that faces anyone who would be a revolutionary in this country. All of us face the task of standing our received social ideology on its head. When we have done that, there will be time enough to rank ourselves and determine who, if anyone, is to be most trusted in the long haul that follows.

Part 3

Ideological Projects

10

Ideology — Under R for Revolution

In this section, I want to talk about ideology and ideological projects, but I do so with some uneasiness. My uneasiness comes from the fact that most of us have a very abstract idea of what ideology is, which we combine with a deep anti-ideological bias that we inherited from the society. The two of course are related. We think of ideology as a musty, nineteenth-century sort of thing that was European in origin and purpose until taken over recently by Third World countries who use it to exorcise American imperialism. And regardless of how we feel about imperialism, our sense of ideologies is that they are rigid, closed, religious in character and sectarian in effect — that is, they make false separations among people. All of this supports and to a certain extent is fostered by our anti-ideological bias — until one day we reach the point of political frustration where suddenly the idea of a rigid (well-worked-out), closed (self-confident), religious (authoritative), sectarian (distinguishing us once and for all from all of them) system becomes terribly appealing. In that situation, which more and more people are experiencing, it seems to be the curse of the Left to immediately rush to the library, check out as many volumes of Lenin's collected works as are available (smirking at the librarian's raised eyebrows), and set to work to give that venerated saint yet another face-lift. It is not that I have anything against Lenin. God forbid! What upsets me is the assumption that those musty books, even if they are correct in every didactic thing they say, can ever substitute for the creation of an ideology out of our own, immediate, verifiable experience. To arrive at Leninism out of our own experience is conceivable and, if it happens, appropriate, but to look for it in the card catalog under "Revolution" is irrelevant and silly.

By now it should be clear that my notions of ideology are a good deal more diffuse than generally accepted. I have talked about "middle-class social ideology" and "working-class social ideology," and if you stick around to the end of this section, I will even talk about a "mass-culture social ideology." Furthermore, I do not see a distinction between "social ideology" and the "political ideologies" we normally associate with the word ideology. Both are basically descriptions of what the world is like and how, in the face of that reality, to proceed with the problem of being alive. It is possible, I suppose, to argue that social ideology, in the sense I have used it, is a description of the way things are, whereas political ideology is a description of how things should be, but I think that is tenuous. Both are both. When I talk about "middle-class social ideology," I am talking about what the middle class "stands for," not necessarily what it is — witness the observation that every child eventually makes about his parents — that they don't live by the values they prescribe. Nor is change by any means the exclusive domain of political ideologies. Middle-class social ideology has very strong notions about change (progress, personal mobility) even if we are inclined to call those ideas the status quo. If you are beginning to be confused at this point, that is fine, because what I really want to do is warn people away from the semantic and psychological snake pit of thinking of political and social ideology as two different things, and recruit you to my more general notion that ideology is anything that deals, more or less coherently (not necessarily consistently or logically), with what the world is like and how to approach the problem of being alive.

The reason all this is important is that so many of us believe we can make a decision whether or not to be "ideological." We assume that ideology is a dusty shelf in the library frequented by archivists and politicos. But it is simply not true. Life is an ideological trip. We are surrounded by ideology — most of which masquerades as something else — but all of which works on us and shapes and limits our sense of the world and what can be done in it. It is true we can pretend that ideology is found only in libraries and SDS meetings, but we cannot avoid the consequence of that pretense, which is acceptance of the cultural lobotomy I call received social ideology.

I have two basic concerns here. First that we expose — make transparent, clear and vivid — the social ideology that was foisted on us, because until we make what is now unconscious, conscious and clear, it is foolish to think that we can imagine anything new that will not be shaped by our unexplored involvement in the old ideological system. Much of this book, and in particular the chapter "We Are Not Middle-Class," is an attempt to make some of that clear. The second thing we must do is understand the converse of what I just said — that is, we will make only limited progress in exposing our current ideological fetters until we have opened up contrasting, new, ideological territory. We need a place to go where we can get distance and perspective on where we are now. We need to climb out of the pit we're in, but we can't climb on thin air; we have to build a ladder. It is this process that I talked about earlier in the chapter on separatism. When a black man realizes that he is beautiful he realizes, simultaneously, that it was somebody else who made him feel ugly. When we make new ideological space, we finally get a handle on the old. And it is the making of new ideological space that must be for now and for the immediately foreseeable future our primary task. Without enough of it, all our organization and action must, in the end, be turned in upon itself.

But how do we begin to think of ourselves as the creators of ideological space — or, for that matter, how do we learn to recognize and claim the space we have already created? If the answer is not found in the card catalog under "R," where is it found? And the answer to that is, all around us. We are surrounded by and to a certain extent involved in many ideologies. What we must learn to do is think about them in the ways that they reflect on, or are part of, our experience. Or said another way, what we must do is learn to reason out of our own experience. And we can reason out of our experience only when we are no longer divorced from it, only when we have begun to be vividly connected to it. Part of the way back into our own experience is to understand how its meaning has been twisted and used against us, and that can really only happen when we recognize the ideologies that have shaped what we call reality.

In this section, I want to talk about my relationship to three different ideologies, or, as I call them, ideological projects. In large part I am doing this to make specific what I have just generalized — to make clearer the way I think about ideology. The three projects (the Economic Research and Action Project of SDS, Women's Liberation, and youth culture) are not at first glance easily related to one another. My relationship to each of them is quite different, and they are each quite different from each other in shape and form. But they are all about ideology even though none of them (with the possible exception of Women's Liberation) really sees itself that way. And they each have much to say, directly or implicitly, about the way we have developed new ideology so far and the direction we should move from here.

11

The Economic Research and
Action Project

The Economic Research and Action Project (ERAP) began in the summer of 1964. For most people it will be remembered as Mississippi Freedom Summer, the summer a thousand white kids went down South to help their black brothers, the summer Schwerner and Goodman (and that other kid — what was his name?) got killed, the summer the Mississippi Freedom Democratic Party challenged the white party from Mississippi at the Democratic Convention (and lost), and of course the summer LBJ was nominated to save us from Goldwater and American boys from dying in a war Asian boys should be fighting. It was still almost a year till the Berkeley uprisings that would result in the arrest of eight hundred at Sproul Hall, and the first major antiwar demonstration, the SDS march on Washington in the spring of 1965, was still a year away.

SDS in fact was still quite a small organization with twenty or thirty chapters and less than a thousand members. It was a fairly impressive feat then for such a small organization to recruit, "train" and place about one hundred twenty full-time summer organizers in ten cities in the East and Midwest. Quite a few of the recruits were not previously SDS members, and the majority of them had had no previous experience with work of this sort.

The job, roughly defined and most simply stated, was to move into poor neighborhoods and begin to organize people around *economic* grievances. By the end of the first summer, the number of projects had thinned out a good deal, but work continued and was even expanded in several cities. Almost exclusively, the people who worked in the projects were white, college-educated, middle-class dropouts. Although the projects varied from place to place, the general pattern was that people pooled their resources, lived cooperatively, and approached the problem of how to move in the community collectively. My own experience was in Cleveland where along with ten other people I began to work in the Near West Side of the city in a poor, heavily Appalachian, white community. Although my work was interrupted for eight months while I served as SDS president, I was in the community or close to it for two and a half years. What I say in this chapter, although I think it has general reference to ERAP, is based mostly on my experience in Cleveland.

ERAP was an impressive undertaking. It attracted some impressive people, and from time to time it made some impressive claims. It moved many people in and outside of the communities where it worked, but despite its claims and accomplishments, three years after its inception it had pretty much disappeared. There are still numbers of "ERAP people" in the five communities where it was strongest (Cleveland, Chicago, Boston, Newark and Baltimore), but the projects they were involved in in every case dissolved into a number of other things, none of which really replaced the original program. I should note here that three years is about a dozen times the normal half-life of political ventures on the New Left, and the fact that there are people "still around" and working in those situations after six years has no parallel in our short history. Nonetheless, virtually everyone involved with ERAP in any way would agree that there were some important failings. For the goal of ERAP was not to survive; it was to transform America. It's objective was not longevity; it was to build a base of mass radical insurgency.

It is important to stress that ERAP's problems were ideological as opposed to practical or even analytical. That is, ERAP's problems did not stem from a lack of skill, imagination, organizing ability, courage, discipline, sex, money or drugs. All of these things and others, more or less, at one time or another, in one project or in all, singly or in combination, did present problems. But studying these problems does not provide the key to understanding ERAP's failings. For on the whole, the people who made up ERAP were exceptionally competent, highly motivated, determined and the rest. So the problem was not a group of people incapable of overcoming practical difficulties.

This is important to underscore because from inside an ERAP project, the most immediate feeling was that there was an overwhelming stream of practical problems, both for us and the people we were working with in the community. The stream of problems was real, and it never let up. One day it was cops harrassing people in the neighborhood who had associated with the project. How do you deal with that? Then next, there is the fight between two critical people in the building you've been trying to organize for a rent strike for the last two months, each of whom insists he will quit if the other does not. What do you do about that? Furthermore, you discover that what triggered the fight was an argument about the nature of the project itself. One woman insisted that we were all Communists, living together in sin and trying to exploit the suffering of the people in the neighborhood and insisted that we should be thrown out of the building. The other points out that nothing would have happened in the building if we hadn't come around in the first place, and insists that we are just decent kids trying to help out people who are worse off. The woman who is "attacking" us is more accurate in her understanding of what we are about than the woman who is "defending" us; what do you do about that? Then there is the man whose family is on relief, who wants to work with you, but is afraid to because he holds a part-time job on the sly, has an ugly caseworker who'd like to get him off relief, and fears that any open involvement with us will draw attention to his case, lead to a discovery of the job and expulsion from the relief roles; what do you do about that? Then of course there is the extraordinary tension between two of the most effective staff members, that no one can quite decipher or bring into the open, but that makes everyone tense and meetings unbearable. Or finally, there is the rather basic fact that the rent is due, the pantry is reduced to peanut butter and pinto beans, and there is ten dollars in the bank with no more in sight for a couple of weeks. What do you do about that — besides develop a sense of humor?

There is no denying that these problems have considerable weight and will demand a lot of energy. Nor is the list I've constructed an exaggeration; it is an ordinary, inelegant piece of life that could have happened to any project in any week, plus frequently a good deal more. However, I've outlined a few of the problems here to draw your attention to two things. First, it is rather suspect to call these "practical" problems. All of them are of course practical in the sense that they arise in a specific situation, demand immediate attention, and have very practical, discernible consequences for your work. But it is also clear that if you push the implications of any of the problems very far, you come to much deeper questions about the nature of your work. For example, the argument between the two women in the rent-strike organization must raise the question of how the project represents itself in the community, how it describes the nature of its work, whether the description it gives of itself (its public line) is truthful. And how do you answer those questions without in turn examining the whole framework of your activity — that is, how do you deal with "practical" problems without getting into their ideological implications? The answer to the last question is, unfortunately, that somehow you *do* manage to look only at the practical aspects of problems or probe only a little bit beneath the surface.

Or to put it another way, we can easily recognize important differences in the way people deal with practical problems. At one extreme, people develop a rich sense of the textured absurdity of life — bitch, moan, hustle, lose sleep and weight — but get by. At another, the same people, or different people with the same problems, are consumed and overwhelmed by them. We normally account for such differences with the rather ephemeral surface information that is available. But in fact, the difference is almost always deeper — is ideological in character. In one situation, the *framework* from which people approached the problem (explicit or implicit) was adequate to provide a practical solution. In another, it was not.

The gist of what I'm writing here was apparent to people in ERAP. There were many occasions when people did feel overwhelmed by the press of practical problems and literally longed for a way of getting at the deeper issues that connected those problems. But somehow, no matter how long the staff meetings and evaluation sessions, it was the press of the immediate, the structuring of the present by the rush of events, that claimed the vast proportion of the energy of ERAP organizers.

Let me add two footnotes here. First, difficulties came not only from practical *problems* but from practical *success*. For example, you finally get people in the building to stop bickering among themselves and you win the rent strike. Everyone is delighted, but only a couple of "organizational types" are interested in coming to meetings any more; now what? Or the welfare grievance procedure you develop is so successful that lots of people start coming to your welfare rights organization for help. You find that you are spending all your time processing welfare grievances — acting in the way a good caseworker should. But that isn't what you really wanted to do. You are overwhelmed by your success. The only way to keep from being destroyed by this kind of success is to have some ideological framework that allows you to make sense of it.

Second, what I am describing is an example of a very universal experience that affects us all in our personal lives, in or out of politics. There are times when the practical problems we face begin to be so heavy that we cannot get beyond them, gain insight into them, regardless of how insignificant they seem — for instance, studying for an exam, writing a letter home, getting the house cleaned up. There are other times when we seem to be able to handle any amount of shit — write six papers in six days, appease our parents for our lack of communication, stop smoking, and make graduate school applications all at the same time. In the first case we are unable to "get a handle on things"; in the second, we have a "steady grip"; the thing we have a grip on or are trying to get hold of, we say is "life." The thirst to find a way to get hold of life, to get a grip on it, to find a framework in which to approach it, is a thirst for *ideology*.

Just as for individuals, there were times for ERAP organizers or projects as a whole when practical problems were handled in stride. Still, in the life of ERAP, practical problems seem to stand out in much sharper relief and with more frequency than they do in the lives of most individuals. The difference is of course that most of our lives are more or less thoroughly structured by a received ideology which automatically and for the most part unconsciously handles innumerable practical matters for us. The times when practical matters seem most difficult are times when that received ideology is being questioned or when it is unable to provide an answer to some life issue we must face.

But ERAP was a self-conscious construction in which a group of people extended themselves into a new social and political dimension. The result had to be an intensification of practical problems, but that intensification itself was the result of an ideological quest.

All of this suggests that it is critical to understand the ideological framework that ERAP projects worked from if we are to understand the difficulties people had in solving "practical problems." One of the reasons for choosing ERAP as an example is because it did make explicit ideological/political statements about itself which in a rough sense can be measured or judged on the basis of their applicability to the concrete problems people came up against.

By far the most important piece of thinking that influenced ERAP's development was a document called "The Interracial Movement of the Poor." Although a lot of people had reservations about the paper, it did summarize and clarify better than anything else the political ideas that ERAP grew out of.

"The Interracial Movement of the Poor" was hardly the most refreshing document to come out of the New Left. Grossly summarized, it made three points: First, it argued that besides black people, there were lots of other kinds of poor people in the United States, all of whom had substantial grievances which potentially they could be organized around. Second, it tried to prove that their ranks were about to be greatly increased as a result of widespread automation, creating an economic crisis of a traditional sort (mass unemployment) which traditional methods would not be able to resolve. Third, it concluded that these factors opened the way for building an interracial movement of the poor around economic issues. Implicit in the third point is a critique of SNCC and the civil rights movement for organizing around the divisive issue of race that separated potential white allies from the movement. However, the paper seemed to accept the challenge that it was up to us to demonstrate that whites could be organized, could make a coalition worthwhile to black people.

This summary makes the paper seem thinner than it was — although it was mighty thin. And generally it is this thinness that people pounce on when they are criticizing the politics of ERAP — particularly the assumption of the paper that simply because people were in bad straits and had grievances they could be organized, and the argument that the cybernetic revolution was going to produce mass unemployment. But these things, to me at least, were not the major weaknesses of the document. For that matter, if the end of the war and increased pressures to automate were to produce a depression during the next few years, people would immediately call the paper prophetic. Mighty movements have frequently been built on very thin (read simple, basic) arguments.

For me, the major shortcoming of "The Interracial Movement of the Poor" analysis was that it was not *our* analysis. It was not what we believed. It did not represent our political vocabulary or our political understanding of the world. It had very little to do with them. In the first place, virtually no one in SDS knew anything about automation. Second, we knew even less about poverty. Our only contact with poverty was through Michael Harrington (*The Other America*) or in some cases through the poor kid and his family we accidentally got to know in high school. Some of us had had contact with black people through the movement, but we had been so caught up in responding to race that we had yet to take deep notice of the other issues in their lives.

What "The Interracial Movement of the Poor" did have that I think we were all looking for was the proper nineteenth century form. It dealt fairly well with our rather stereotyped ideas about what a political statement should be like. It had an "economic analysis," which as we all know is the most grisly kind of analysis you can have. It identified and described an "agency" or class (the poor) whose grievances were *objectively* ripe for radical action. And it made beginning hypotheses about a strategy of action and change. In short, the document dealt with the "big questions" in the proper form and that was in some sense more important than the content of what it said.

What we really needed a document for was not to deal with the poor but to deal with us. We needed it to pry ourselves away from the comfortable middle-class careers and circumscribed lives we were scheduled by the society to lead. In order to shake ourselves loose, I think most of us needed a political analysis that was bold (arrogant) enough to assert that through its implementation we could change America. That is to say, in order to give our full energy to something, we needed an analysis that would allow us to take seriously our very deep feeling that the country had to be changed radically. We also needed a political program that promised to link us to the black movement. Any set of ideas that failed to make that connection would have failed to connect in our eyes with the only demonstrable revolutionary potential that existed in the country.

But our whole sense of the way *relevant* connections were made was very abstract. It went almost without saying that a political analysis that was any "good" would be intuitively incomprehensible. However, given this framework of thinking, "The Interracial Movement of the Poor" document accomplished its main political tasks more than adequately. Not only did it promise to change America, but it promised eventual political and organizational ties with black militance.

However, once these political ideas got us out of Ann Arbor and Swarthmore, they began to be counterproductive. In the first place, they were simply inaccurate as a description of what was going on in America. We were not met by armies of white unemployed, and the unemployed we did meet were an extremely disparate group of people. There were winos, old people on relief and fixed pensions, young guys who still hadn't adjusted to the notion that they would spend their lives marketing themselves to factory owners, and older, steady workers who were laid off or "temporarily out of work." Making these people into one organization of unemployed to demand jobs from a cybernating economy that could not provide them was far and away tougher than convincing any group of them that black people were not their enemies. The fact that they were all unemployed or underemployed was a strange common denominator for one of the most variegated groups I can imagine. To top it all off, when the ERAP projects began, unemployment was actually decreasing in most of the cities we worked in.

The discrepancy between fact and analysis set off a rather forlorn, funny debate during the first summer, known as "JOIN versus GROIN." JOIN stands for Jobs or Income Now, the demand and the name of the Chicago union of unemployed workers; GROIN or Garbage Removal or Income Now was the acronym thought up by somebody in Chicago to describe the rapidly developing tendency in most projects to ignore the hard-core issue of jobs. People who took the JOIN position said we had to stick by our analysis no matter how difficult the organizational job, and make the basic demand, the Achilles' heel of the society, visible and militant. GROIN people, who were insulted by the tone of the acronym, defended themselves on the "practical" basis that jobs just weren't the issue to move people on, and counterattacked against JOIN people for still not providing a scheme for organizing around jobs.

In the end, of course, GROIN "won," but it was a sad kind of victory. For the tone of the debate had been to characterize the JOIN people as the hard-nosed, hard-core, principled ideologues and the GROIN folks as somewhat softer, humanistic, pragmatist revisionists. Not only was the political idea JOIN stood for weakened, but the whole efficacy of conscious ideological thinking suffered as well. More than before, people began to think of their work as a pragmatic experiment divorced from any clear ideological propositions. This tendency, which to a certain extent had existed all along, was to grow stronger the longer the ERAP projects existed.

To put it another way, ERAP people were still operating out of the assumption that we could choose whether or not to be ideological. We still thought of ideology as an academic, self-conscious construction that made abstractions about the world. We failed to understand that ideology is immediate and pervasive and that the relevant ideological task is to understand the ideologies that shape your most intimate feelings about yourself and your environment.

Essentially the new "pragmatic" idea that replaced "The Interracial Movement of the Poor" was that you find out what people's troubles are and you organize them around that. The new slogans were "no rent for rats," "adequate welfare now," "end police brutality," and above all, "let the people decide." We were more comfortable with the new ideas, not only because they allowed us to move and work, but because in some ways they were closer to our own, more intuitively comprehended ideas. "Let the people decide" is about democracy and people controlling their own lives, and that after all was a cornerstone of our intuitive politics. But the trouble was that we had reduced a complicated political idea to a slogan, and the slogan was inadequate; it left us rudderless since we were trying to figure out its meaning for other people, instead of ourselves.

I want to stress again that the major weakness of "The Interracial Movement of the Poor" idea was not its inadequacies and inaccuracies analytically. Its major weakness was that it did not deal with the ideological problem of the people, the ERAP staff, who "subscribed" to it and lived under it. It did not expose or explore our received social ideology. Rather, it deflected us from that exploration by focusing our attention on "the poor." It did not make new ideological space for us. It was not an ideology we *could* live under, witness the fact that it almost completely washed away with the first rain. It was not an ideology that we could internalize, because it was not about our insides. Had it been that, we might have revised it, corrected its rigidities or eliminated some of its sloppiness — in short, have struggled to evolve our political understanding of the world. Instead, by and large, we caved in and gave up that part of the struggle for the increasingly more pressing struggle of keeping afloat in the communities where we had chosen to live and work.

How did it happen? To me at least, it seems in retrospect that the interracial movement of the poor idea was a paste-up, a bunch of ideas that were strung together to justify — give weight and stature to — what a lot of people felt in their gut. I think people felt the middle class would never make it, that our sector of the society was not going to produce a revolution, and that we had to split with it. Closely connected to that feeling was the sense that somewhere else in the society people with *legitimate* grievances were getting creamed and would be willing to stand up and fight with *us*. Both italicized words are important, because there was a deep inner conviction that *our* grievances were not legitimate (the middle class would not produce the revolution), and therefore our concern with social change could only be authentic if tied to people whose struggle *was* legitimate — people who were getting creamed.

Those gut feelings, which never got explicitly discussed, were a hangover from our own guilt-ridden liberal identities. They had been exacerbated a lot by the tensions with SNCC which heightened our guilt and our feelings of inauthenticity. They were heightened as well by the shallowness of the commitment we felt in people all around us — and perhaps — who could be sure — in ourselves. For us, the trajectory our lives were cut out to follow was one of personal comfort and compromise. We "knew" that we could be extremely competent cop-outs. For our black and poor contemporaries, we were led to understand there was an objective impediment to selling out; they, unlike us, were in unending structural opposition to America. A few months later, when we discovered for ourselves that if you're poor in America it takes an unending reserve of energy and courage to do anything *but* sell out, it was too late to make the connection. Because once you were on the frontier, organizing in poor communities, the pressure to backslide into the middle class was more intense than ever and had to be resisted more than ever. And the need to believe that poor people wouldn't sell out, would make the revolution, was greater than ever. After all, we had tied our political dreams to their reality.

"The Interracial Movement of the Poor" document did not really fill a vacuum; rather it succumbed to a psychology that people had been resisting when they wrote the "Port Huron Statement" and the "America and the New Era" document. Both of these were good beginning attempts to define who we were and what we were angry about. They were broad cultural, political and economic documents. In contrast, the ERAP doctrine was a narrow economic analysis. It talked about one "class," a funny class at that, called "the poor." And it failed to talk about even that class in a dynamic way;

it communicated no sense of the involvement of the poor with groups or institutions in the society or with the society as a whole. As a static analysis, it could offer no projection about how the conflict between poor people and the institutions that oppressed them might develop over time. In short, ERAP substituted a kind of closed, vulgar Marxism for the more hopeful tentativeness of earlier SDS proclamations. And it was clear that many people in ERAP felt that the two sets of ideas could not coexist. Their attitude seemed to be that the "Port Huron Statement" had simply been a kind of simpy, rhetorical exercise that had covered up or masked the hard, crisp, basic economic analysis that was now emerging.

Everything that I've said so far should suggest the variety and the enormity of the pressures that led to the vulgarization of both the New Left and Marx — the pressures from the black movement, doubts we had about our own legitimacy and commitment, the need to define a way to change America and specify agencies of that change, the availability of money for economic research and action (what if somebody had allotted dough for cultural research and action?), etc. But it would be very wrong to assume that those pressures — the pressures to disbelieve the validity of your own experience — were unique to ERAP. They are always present, and they are certainly present today — if anything more intensely. All of them tend to control our ideas and distort their development. And resisting those pressures is very difficult. Being acutely aware of their presence and acknowledging their significance is the first vital task. ERAP never accomplished it.

Let me spell out a bit more clearly the political tasks the interracial movement of the poor idea did not accomplish. First, it did not deal with who we were politically. If poor people were going to make the revolution, then who were the middle-class people who came to work with them? The implication of the ERAP analysis was that we were catalysts, the neutral agent that facilitates a reaction it is not a part of, that is not latent in it. It is incredible that we could create a political ideology and not give ourselves even superficial examination, but that is exactly what we did.

Second, it did not specify or conceptualize, even in our role as catalyst, how we were to make a connection between ourselves and the people we were supposed to work with. How does a catalyst organize? What does he do with the conflict between himself and the community?

Third, it did not locate us in political time and space, and in failing to do that, failed to give a sense to people in ERAP of what portion of the burden of history they were supposed to carry. This is important to understand. By political time and space, I mean that every ideology must understand something about its own development, where it and the movement it speaks for have been in the past and where they should expect to be in the future. That understanding is the only thing that gives people a sense of what their role is and what their priorities are, short of the immediate accomplishment of the revolution. We needed to have a feeling for what stage of development our movement was at, a sense of how it was formed and unformed. Was ERAP the last stage, the model of organizational development that would lead directly to political power? Or did we expect to evolve something else beyond ERAP, a political party or a terrorist organization? What connection did ERAP have to SDS politics before it? Was it an affirmation of them? A rejection of them?

Finally, part of finding your location in political time and space is to know how you feel about groups and movements outside your immediate political sphere. Can you expect help from any place else or must ERAP carry the whole burden of history with a little help from SNCC? In fact, people in ERAP seemed to share a pessimism about what other people were doing, or perhaps I should say, a false sense of self-importance about their own work. The price you pay for that sense of self-importance, the sense that your little movement is the cutting edge, *the* critical instrument for change, is an immediate sense of isolation, an awareness of your minute size and power. This too was a reversal of earlier SDS political analysis, which in most respects had been more generous and optimistic. The "America and the New Era" document had talked about a great deal of insurgency developing in the United States, and although not specifically endorsing most of it, had seen positive elements and trends in much of what was going on, had found reason to be hopeful that events were leading all kinds of people to similar conclusions about the country. The ERAP ideology, by not discussing our relationship to other groups in the society and by putting so much emphasis on community organizing as *the* way, implicitly made us hostile to other groups and movements.

The way in which the interracial movement of the poor idea closed and narrowed our thinking had a number of destructive effects. The only real political role it created was that of the catalyst/organizer of the poor; if you couldn't make that, then you just couldn't make it. It segmented the movement more internally, and in general, increased the feeling of isolation on the Left, particularly within ERAP. It reduced a broad cultural, political and economic analysis to a narrow economic analysis that few people could authentically identify with. It reduced the capacity of ERAP staff for making political judgments by making them auxiliary and ancillary to another group. It escalated the image of the importance of ERAP to such an extent that ERAP staff simply had to buckle under the great weight of history they had to carry.

In contrast, it should be perfectly clear by now that I feel that the more honest (self-aware), deliberate vagueness of an earlier New Left analysis would have been a sounder ideological insight to depart from. Suppose for a moment that the people and energy that went into ERAP had been devoted to a more general project to deepen, expand, develop and refine the political ideas of the "Port Huron Statement" and "America and the New Era." Not only do I feel that would have been a more genuine expenditure of ourselves, but (in retrospect) it seems clear that it was the kind of project that was needed. Thousands of people were beginning to flow into the movement, many of them initially attracted by the promise of the radical analysis SDS had done. What was needed was a sharpening of many facets of the analysis that had attracted them. We had to learn how and why we were connected to the problems we kept talking about.

But people in SDS, through the interracial movement of the poor ideology, had seen a chance to go directly for the jugular vein of the system. We leapt and missed and came up, not with a new society, but with a slightly different portion of the well-chewed piece of gristle so many American radicals had gnawed and choked on before.

After this much criticism, most people would conclude, I suppose, that I consider ERAP to have been a rather enormous failure. ERAP's failures were numerous and extensive and, as I hope this chapter has shown, I am not in the least interested in denying them. But in the very relative scale by which achievements in a still young Left movement must be measured, I find ERAP made a very important contribution to the development of the movement.

Despite its ideological fogginess, it was the closest thing we've had yet to a conscious ideological project. A group of people tried to formulate a set of political ideas and implement them systematically. The very fact that ERAP can be criticized so extensively speaks to its ideological attempt, and in that sense, it did make new ideological space, even if hindsight suggests it was a tangent. It physically and emotionally dislocated people from their moorings around the university. It implemented our need to move out and explore. It left us with a new body of experience (no matter how mind-boggling) to make sense of. It created a structure of ideas and a clear record of attempts to implement them that is available to us to understand. Most projects on the Left are so *ad hoc* in their definition and so undernourished in their implementation that it is impossible to have any clear sense of what went wrong or right — evaluation itself must be *ad hoc*. That keeps the Left on the knee-jerk level of development, and although it's possible that the knee will someday jerk the foot into some vital part of the system, I for one will not hold my breath.

And although in retrospect the ERAP program seems to have missed the mark very widely, it might be an even greater mistake to reject the positive elements of that failure. The Canton workers' commune was crushed decisively. And Castro's first mad attack on Cuba was a horrendous fiasco. In the first case the defeat led to an enormous change in the direction of the revolution. In the second, the same man did essentially the same thing over again and won.

12

Youth Culture

I want to talk about youth culture as an ideological project. But in contrast to ERAP, where I was talking about something with fairly clear limits and definitions in which I was centrally involved, youth culture has many different manifestations, is very diffuse and is something in which I feel myself to be only peripherally involved. But despite its diffuseness, it does seem to me that you can talk about youth culture as a very important, broad, ideological project that in one or another way, everyone in the society has become involved in. At the center, perhaps, are the people living in communes in New Mexico or the street people in Berkeley or the kid panhandling on the Lower East Side or the guy who just tossed his Harvard fellowship in the fire and split. And at the other end are the Attorney General and the President down in the war room trying to plug up the Mexican border so that nobody can smoke dope and trying to figure out how they're going to bribe the Mexican government to use all the great weapons the United States perfected in Vietnam to run a guerrilla war against the marijuana plant. And in between, strung out from the war room to New Mexico, are all the rest of us who have different relationships to this very broad and diffuse, but very real thing, called youth culture. I suppose you could even get into an argument about who really constitutes the center of youth culture so that some people might want to put the Beatles and Janis Joplin and Peter Fonda and Allen Ginsberg and Tim Leary and Ken Kesey and all the other hip stars in the middle since they are so important. However, I would not want to put them there, but I also would not want to argue about it very much, since, as I said in the beginning, we are talking about something very diffuse. It is not important to come up with an accurate diagram of youth culture, but rather, it is important to be able to talk about what your real relationship is to what you think youth culture is. And that is what I want to talk about because although my relationship to youth culture is general and eclectic and consists mostly of people I have met and things I have felt, it is quite important to me and leads me to feel that there are some things I want to say, even though they are said at a greater distance from the hypothetical center of youth culture than I wish they were.*

* This is also a comment about the nature of an ideological project, because a project does send out waves from its center that reach many people who are not intensely involved in it (this was true of ERAP), and regardless of whether those waves are accurate representations of what is going on at the center, people can and do have very real relationships that can change their lives with what they perceive is going on. And this in turn presents the people who are consciously and intensely concerned with an ideological problem with the question of whether or not they want to worry about those waves in the sense of trying to portray them-

The first thing I want to say is that youth culture seems to me to speak most clearly to the needs of men as opposed to the needs of women, which does not mean that it does not have very important implications for women. Viewed from even the most superficial life-style level, men are not only allowed to wear long hair and jewelry and things that were previously preserved for women, but what is more important, they are permitted to look really freaky and scary and act that way too. Whereas women are still supposed to look lovely and soft and demure and have certain kinds of passive smiles and gestures that when you think about it are still very hooked up with the idea of what a woman is in this society. There is some liberation for women. They are allowed to dress and look natural and not wear makeup and bras or high heels or any of the other more obvious symbols of self-destruction other women are supposed to lay themselves under. But it is clear, despite all this, that women are still supposed to look a certain way, namely attractive and sensual to men, and this idea is not a bit different from the social mandate that forces other women to be subservient to cosmetics and fashion.

Most centrally and positively, what youth culture means to me is an attempt to release men from some of the enormous male ego burden this society has placed upon them. The youth culture drug experience helps men relax and open up with one another and ease away some of the brittle, rigid, defensive/ competitiveness they normally experience whenever they are together. The freedom to stop constantly propping up the male ego (even in your fantasies) that comes from this opening, is the freedom for men to begin to inhabit their own minds. The capacity men feel to get involved in themselves is almost directly proportional to the softening they feel in their armor, the easing away of the constant tension and anxiety about ade-

selves accurately to people who are interested, or whether they feel it is just too difficult to worry about how the reality of their experience gets filtered out as it gets pushed along the cultural grapevine.

quacy, the opening up of gentle feelings — a softening toward themselves.

Oddly enough, this is why I think so many men wind up ego tripping on drugs. For the first time in their lives, they feel relaxed and open enough about themselves to really enjoy being themselves, to really project themselves without the old vain fear of exposing weakness. It is not quite that the vanity disappears; rather, it becomes easier to inform the vanity that it has been much too nervous, and to assure yourself that you really are quite a fine fellow, even if some of the weakness shows, and to assume that everyone else will see this too.

For some there is temporary escape from the tyranny of defending masculine ego, and it opens up for the first time the possibility that they can become deeply involved in something or someone outside of themselves without losing track of themselves. Some of these men seem to have really almost lost a male ego and are on the edge of coming to a totally new sense of themselves. And they are the ones who seem to me to be most profoundly involved in youth culture (which is why I didn't want the stars in the middle).

For a long time, I was puzzled by the fact that I kept meeting these two rather contradictory kinds of men — men who were ego tripping intensely in one way or another, and men who seemed out of touch with their male ego. But slowly I've begun to understand the connection between the two; finally not having to be afraid to ego trip and finally getting a chance to expend all that frightened, vain energy, allows men some freedom to explore other ways of relating to the world and themselves. Protecting male ego took nine-tenths of the energy. Letting it run frees up other potential — helps men get beyond the constant sex-role tension their lives are supposed to balance on.

Women, who have the other end of the ego problem, are much more frequently, in my experience, seriously freaked or made to feel schizophrenic by drugs, or conversely, are much less involved and interested in the drug experience. It's as if drugs are more fitted to male needs — or perhaps I should say the drug culture or youth culture is.

Because I do not believe that drugs are mystical. The real thrust behind youth culture is the collapse of American moral hegemony this generation has witnessed most dramatically in Vietnam and the American ghettoes — but pretty much everywhere else too. It is this force that is moving many men to see and want to escape the horrendous social roles they are supposed to fill. It is these men in particular who have been attracted to drugs and who have the kind of involvement in youth culture I have described. And there clearly seems to be a kind of class differentiation here, because it does still seem to be preponderantly middle-class men who are involved in drug culture, even though everybody now is involved in drugs. Very significantly, drugs facilitate a process whose origins they do not control.

Stated another way, youth culture has most to do with the conscious inability of growing numbers of men to fit into male roles as they are defined by this society. The intensity of the social sanctions against men who don't make it ("These hippies can't make it — they are barely men at all") may explain why it is so important for dropout men to be surrounded by women who are still fairly traditionally defined — or for that matter, is one of the reasons it is important for them to be involved with women at all. It is one thing to experiment with your male ego. It is quite another to gratuitously put your balls on the chopping block. It's quite possible to stomach all the epithets and derision and keep coming back for more, so long as there is a woman and women who know you're a man and let you know it.

Perhaps this last statement about the kind of need there is for women is too harsh, but it is a sense I have sometimes and it speaks very directly to what I said before about youth culture being primarily constructed around the needs of men.

Or to approach this same problem from yet another tack, note that I talked about the *conscious* inability of dropout men to fit into male roles — because I think most dropout men I have met feel that they have made a *decision* to drop out. This implies that they believe, whether it is true or not, that the decision could have been made the other way, or for that matter still could be, and that they could still, if they wanted to, which of course they don't, "make it." To the extent that men still need to feel that they could make it if they wanted to, they still must hang onto their old competitive, aggressive identities and still be able to think of themselves in the good old American way without feeling that they are thinking about someone else. They must still, somewhere deep down, tie their image of themselves to the old society.

All of this connects to the failure of dropout men to realize that they are in serious trouble. Most women, unlike men, are aware that they are in trouble — pretty constant danger — whether that is defined as fear that they might be hurt or ignored at any moment by men or defined as not being able to cope with a situation or ever have orgasm or not being able to "control" their emotions — women do have this sense of being in trouble and vulnerable. But most men do not. They try to feel "in control of themselves" — believe they can make decisions about how they will spend their lives — that is, by deciding whether or not to "make it."

The ramifications of this small point, when you think about it, are vast. Because if you must always assure yourself that you could make it, even if it is only at the back of your mind, then you can never let the milieu you are in develop into one which would convince you that you *couldn't* make it — which means you must find some way to express your allegiance to the old society in the way you live. But if you are trying at the same time to convince yourself that you've split with the old ways (and many of us are), then you must find a way to show this allegiance without really acknowledging to yourself that you are — which is a kind of elaborate trick you wind up playing on yourself. Or if you do acknowledge begrudgingly that you haven't been able to make the split, you feel guilty and middle-class and "self-indulgent." Whereas a man who did really believe that he couldn't make it — could never sell a car or work in a factory or teach in a school or fuck a woman — would in fact realize that he was in very serious trouble and would therefore have a chance — would almost be forced to try to find out what the trouble was — find out what the real nature of his oppression was.

This is a very critical element of what I feel about youth culture. Although it is built around the needs of men, primarily white middle-class men, it has still not made a clear break with old definitions. It may strike you that I am being picayune, since at another intuitive level it does seem clear that large segments of the youth culture really have made a sharp break with the society. And although I want to acknowledge that break and do not want to detract from its importance unnecessarily, I do think this small point is very critical. It is the difference between feeling your life is a "style" or a posture and feeling that your life is an expression of who you are. At its core, it is the difference between feeling legitimate and illegitimate. It is the difference between feeling like a timid freak or feeling like a just madman. And it adds up to being very decisive in determining how you will spend your energy — whether it will be spent in identifying and resisting your oppression, or whether it will be used defensively to ward off certain questions that are too dangerous to ask.

But it is important to recognize that it is within the youth culture that you can find middle-class people who are looking most seriously at their own oppression. And that gives it much more human, revolutionary potential than the organized movement at this point. Viewed as an ideological project, youth culture has created a great deal of space where people can get away from some of the most direct pressures created by jobs and schools and polite, well-dressed society and look at what they are about. But even though I believe it is exciting, and even though I believe the dynamics of youth culture, despite all sorts of attempts at co-optation, is moving toward more profound self-recognition, I still do have the feeling that youth culture has concentrated its attention on the wrong thing.

It seems to me that youth culture is looking at *mass culture* when at the very least it should be looking at middle-class culture. This takes more words to explain than I think it should, but if you will try to follow it, I think it is important. By mass culture I mean the more or less pervasive symbols this society projects of itself through TV and advertising and textbooks and union officials and judges and movies and Congress and other agencies, all of which are characterized by having highly universal access to people, and by the fact that they are constantly involved in creating a mass social ideology (mythology) about America. When I talk about the breakdown of American "moral hegemony," I mean specifically the civics-books social ideology I call here mass culture. I use the term "mass culture" as opposed to "middle-class culture" or "working-class culture" precisely because these other social ideologies are generated out of the problems and experience of a particular class or group, whereas the social ideology generated by mass culture applies more or less pervasively to all groups in the society.

Just to make this distinction clearer, one of the ways to note the difference between mass culture and middle-class culture is that so many middle-class people are onto mass America, have become aware of how superficial and vacuous and plastic the country is, and how banal the rhetoric of politicians and judges is, and how stupid and inaccurate the textbooks are, without in any way getting close to the nature of their own oppression or even beginning to make a break with their own class arrogance and social ideology. In fact, from the point of view of maintaining the existing order, one way of looking at the "function" of mass culture is that it distracts people from zeroing in on their own oppression by involving them in contending, in extremely class-biased ways, over how the mass culture is to be represented. To use another example from another class, many of the adherents of George Wallace supported his campaign because he represented to them, in almost exactly the same way McCarthy did to the intelligentsia, an attempt by a "little man" to contend with the symbols and rhetoric of mass culture. One very important effect of mass culture is that it strengthens allegiances to status quo, class-based social ideologies, while buffering class antagonisms and giving them an arena in which they can be played out fairly harmlessly — harmless because, as we have seen many times, the tone of mass culture can change without loosening the subservience of any class to its oppressive social ideology. So that even if enough social pressure was brought to bear and the Smothers Brothers won their fight to stay on TV, or the FCC makes the networks do more cultural programming, nothing much has happened other than a certain class group getting better representation for its prejudices in the mass culture, which again, as we know, is a trend that could easily be reversed.

Now what all this has to do with youth culture is that we confuse mass culture and middle-class culture — which is easy to do given the generally accepted tendency by almost everybody to associate everything American with the middle class. One of the ways the middle class disguises itself is to pretend that it is everything from McDonald's Hamburgers to the Chase Manhattan Bank. It is not. It is neither of those things and it is not a lot of other things it usually gets pegged as being. It is a much more specific set of things and values which I attempted to outline earlier. Our confusion allows us to denounce plastic America with vehemence while ignoring the inbred competitiveness among ourselves. Or worse yet, it allows us to denounce Lyndon Johnson as an ogre while being intrigued with Gene McCarthy.

To take an example that is more directly connected to youth culture, I think one of the things we are onto is the meaninglessness of work. It is an important accomplishment that there exists in the society at this time an ideological project that embodies the notion that work, particularly highly bureaucratized, specialized and mechanized work, is dehumanizing and basically meaningless. And it is understandable, I think, that people should see this attitude toward work as a repudiation of a middle-class value. But it is not. Work is a very important mass-culture value that every boy growing up in this society gets a strong dose of. The unique contribution of middle-class culture to the whole idea of work is not that work is important, although that idea is implicit, but that work is *meaningful* and *creative*, that work is a self-fulfillment project. The repudiation of work is the repudiation of a mass-culture value, not a middle-class value. A lot of kids who have "dropped out" are still very much involved in a search for meaningful work, are still very loyal to the notion that meaningful creative work can and must be found in this society — even if it can only be found "outside" the mainstream. This has led to a very heavy involvement in the crafts and the arts. In fact it is possible to imagine that the final result of the current dropout culture would be the development of a stable, bohemian class of craftsmen, artisans and artists.

For me, that represents an unhappy ending. Because look at what the kid who lives in Vermont and throws pots as a decent way of making a living (that requires the use of his hands and actually has some utility) has to do. He has to protect himself from the insight that the upper-middle-class people who buy and use handmade pots are buying them to decorate their lives and tables and insulate themselves from the knowledge that they live in an utterly sterile world. And it is only

if he can protect himself from the knowledge that he is buffering and making more livable the very things he says he hates,
that he can continue to believe in creative work. Maybe to be
fair, the more important counterexample would be the communes where people only work to subsist and have perhaps
given up on the old middle-class notion of work creativity.
Because I do believe that there are a lot of people inside the
youth culture who are beginning to understand and internalize the fact that this society has undermined and corrupted all
attempts at creative work.

But I still feel that the point I am trying to make about the
importance of seeing the distinction between mass culture and
middle-class culture has general, if not universal, validity. It is
important because I believe the middle class is quite capable
of accepting and profiting from much of the critique of mass
culture implicit in youth culture — a more natural look for
women, relaxation of some sexual hypocrisy, resuscitation of
arts and crafts (now that there is the affluence to make them
profitable), an openness towards drugs, etc.

The very way in which youth culture seems to resist mass
culture suggests that we are looking at the wrong thing. Because the method of resistance seems to be a determination to
swallow mass culture whole. The word for swallowing whole
is "groove." Kids turn the television set into a light show, or
sit on a street corner and watch cars go by all day, or go into
a plastic restaurant and order a cup of coffee and sit for hours
and watch the plastic people come in and out — and all of
these things and many more are a kind of swallowing whole
of the culture in the sense that the whole idea of a TV as a
cultural symbol which has certain meanings attached to it is
consumed. The TV is taken as a whole piece and "grooved
on" in the sense that its essence, its essential quality, is understood apart from its cultural meaning. You swallow a TV by
turning off the sound and crossing up the vertical and hori-
zontal tuning and then turning off the lights and feeling all those

eletrical dots move around inside you; and in doing that, you come as close as you can to comprehending its essence, thus destroying its cultural meaning, or its power as a cultural symbol to oppress you. Similarly with cars or plastic restaurants or city noise levels or work in the post office — any number of things. And I will acknowledge that this is a very important way to see things because it clearly gives you a certain insight into the nature of the way things in your world work on you and it gives you a capacity to survive in that environment by keeping it under penetrating observation.

But what makes me uneasy or makes me feel this is the observation of the wrong things is that I do not think people could keep so cool if they were looking right at the thing that had disfigured them — not if I'm anywhere close to right in my sense of how deeply disfigured we are and how terrible is the recognition of that. And the fantasy it creates in my mind is that I would like to be able to take kids away from grooving on plastic and put them down in front of a village being bombed in Vietnam, or in the middle of a circle of beautiful women chanting "He's not a man, he can't make it," or in front of club-swinging hate-filled cops in Chicago or anywhere, or in the middle of a desert where there is nothing you can do or say that will express yourself, and see whether they could groove on those things. And perhaps people could do that and comprehend the essence of those things and be liberated from their power, but I do not believe it. I do not understand that notion of liberation.

Even the opposite of the notion of grooving — freaked or freaking-out — carries some of its insulation. Because when you can't "groove" on a thing, and it gets to you and you "freak," then you have a kind of crazy, spontaneous reaction to it which allows you to express some of your fear and maybe even anger. So that if you suddenly freaked out in a plastic restaurant, that is, weren't able to swallow it whole, you could easily imagine yourself actually getting up and shouting "All you people are dead, don't you know that?" and seeing people look up from their food and newspapers as if *you* were crazy, just so many dead eyes looking at you with this vacant incomprehension. And again, although the permission to freak out, the notion that it is a reasonable thing to do in such a situation, is very important, and allows people to surface some of their true reactions, it is still thought of as a kind of temporary episode, a kind of momentary, permitted lapse into the reality of how you feel. Because the kid who is permanently and completely freaked-out is crazy, and although there is more tolerance and interest in craziness among dropout people than there is in any other sector of our society, and although there is enormous intellectual curiosity, I sense little ability in hip culture to deal with real madness — to live with it close up rather than trip on about it in order to keep it away. Hip culture is still too cool and superficial to make hard contact with its own emotional crises. So I keep coming back to the feeling that hip culture and hip people are still examining and looking at and grooving on or freaking out on some of the most superficial and distant aspects of their oppression. In some sense, we are waiting for a decision to be made as to whether or not they will be willing to risk getting on about the business of looking deeper into their own oppression, right down inside the maggot-infested wound.

But before I leave the word "groovy" behind, I want to talk about love, because it is true that hip culture is doing something to the notion of love. It is converting love from its old definition to a description of something that is both a basic social and personal need. Because despite quite a bit of bad press on the subject and some fairly innocuous music, I do not believe that most people who are involved in hip culture believe that "love is easy." The pervasive use of the word in hip culture describes mostly the strong sense people have of what is missing and what is potential in human relationships. So when a kid hands you a flower and says "Love," he doesn't quite mean that he loves you, but he does mean that he could have loved you and it would have been easy and natural had things not turned out the way they did. So the flower can be seen as sort of an apology for his complicity in what is going on, and again, as a fairly firm statement about what is potential. Or at least, I feel that is what is happening. So love is pervasively seen and felt as a potential, but the phrase used most frequently to describe good, clear, forceful relationships among people is not that people are "in love" but that they are "really grooving on one another." And grooving means people have found some theme or themes that they are deeply involved in with one another, some way of communicating that is quite important to each or all of them and that they share deeply as a common experience or idea. That experience need not be verbal, because sometimes people can just look at one another, or not even look at each other but just be in the same place, and know that they are reacting the same way, experiencing the same things about each other and the things they are seeing or hearing — really grooving. And what is interesting about this is not that it happens, because these things happen fairly ordinarily to all sorts of people, but that in hip culture that kind of relationship is allowed to happen without becoming obligatory. That is, people can groove on one another without beginning to describe the relationship as a love relationship, without confusing the momentary capacity we have to share things with many people very deeply with a broader, more intensive capacity called love. There is a singularity given to the significance of an experience that does not depend on the experience being repeated. That is, I think there is a recognition implicit in how people relate to one another that love, in the sense of two or more people sharing experience so deeply that they become one, is impossible, and yet at the same time there is this very strong sense that love is real. And this has to be a tremendously liberating notion because it allows people not to pretend at something they cannot be and therefore suffer the consequences of that pretense, but in fact to be what they can — to learn to groove on one another and share the validity and universality of certain experience — to know the potential for love.

It is only here that the distance and detachment that is tied up in the word groovy seems right to me. Because it recognizes how insurmountable the distance that really separates us is, without giving up on it, and the only objection I have to the word in this context is that it is a little bit too cool and does not really acknowledge that people could, in some limited sense, accept a responsibility (exert the will to be alive and available) toward one another.

13

Why I Like Women's Liberation

Perhaps the simplest thing I can say about why I like Women's Liberation is that I believe the closest experience to love I will find with a woman in this society is with a woman who is deeply involved in a struggle for her own liberation. This does not suppose that the struggle must be one called Women's Liberation, because the important thing would not be what name she gave her attempt at liberation, if she gave it any name at all, but rather that she was in fact involved in a struggle for her own liberation and what the experience of this struggle would do to her capacity to have a relationship of integrity with another person. However, since of the women I know who seem involved in a struggle for their own liberation, almost all call that struggle Women's Liberation, I find myself intrigued with what the Women's Liberation movement has to do with my life, and find myself feeling that that movement has become very important to my life.

But when I think about it I do not like the statement I just made. Although it is a true statement, in the sense that it does say what I mean, it also says something else to many people which is not what I mean. There are some men I have met who would make almost the exact same statement I made but for whom it means that "liberated chicks are the grooviest chicks, the most interesting to be with and far and away the best screw"; which is a way of saying that Women's Liberation, along with everything else in this society, is something that can be marketed and consumed, something men can dominate and use. So I am always suspicious of men who say they like Women's Liberation, because I am not sure, until I have talked to them, whether they are simply very clever chauvinists, who are still playing out their role as master objectifiers and consumers in the society (consumers of life, master objectifiers of all things and relationships), or whether they in fact have sensed the revolutionary implications a revolutionary movement must have for all people it comes in touch with. And when I see other men relate to Women's Liberation this way, I can easily recognize in myself this consumer/objectifier capacity. I find myself wondering if I too am simply titillated by Women's Liberation in the sense that my male ego is challenged, leading me to become involved very subtly and insidiously in trying to subvert it. And in fact I realize there have been times in conversations when I have been caught or have caught myself trying to impose my patterns of thinking about Women's Liberation on women so that their movement would be more comprehensible to me, more accessible to me, more manipulatable by me.

So that perhaps the more honest and simple statement I

should make, rather than the statement I first made, is that the reason I like Women's Liberation is because it has taught me to be far more self-conscious of my own chauvinism. This does not mean it allows me to overcome that chauvinism, but it does at least create for me, and for all men who come in contact with it, a situation where the self-recognition of chauvinism could point them in the direction of, force them to be aware of, their own need for liberation. So let me start with this, which is clearer and which I feel more comfortable in saying, and see whether we can work our way back to love.

One of the sad things about the black liberation movement is that because of the almost complete segregation in this society, the instruction it has given has been very remote. The meaning of black liberation has been filtered through newspapers, lecture halls and television documentaries and has been twisted by the distorted recollections of people who have experienced it firsthand but have been unable to come to grips with that experience. So our whole image of black liberation has an abstractness attached to it by the media. It is only a few of the white people who have encountered black liberation close up who have perhaps realized how deeply it implicates everything about their lives, the deepest assumptions of their lives, and have therefore been able to piece together a new sense of themselves from the greater insight these encounters gave. But even then, the value of that experience and the instruction it gives is diminished by the bizarre contexts in which most whites have interaction with black people. It is hard to translate the instruction of black liberation out of such peculiar settings. The abstractness of black liberation is most easily digested if it is thought of in highly intellectualized categories. Thinking in this way creates the superrationalistic tone most of us, and particularly the movement, adopt when talking about black liberation. However for me and many white men, Women's Liberation is very close up and not at all abstract. There is just no way to avoid the question of Women's Liberation in our daily lives, because we know women and keep meeting more women who constantly raise it. Racism is so effectively ghettoized and segregated that we can go for months or years or lifetimes without ever coming face to face with the reality that racism is something that pervades our lives. But that avoidance is just much more difficult with Women's Liberation.

But you will want to know why I think proximity to a Women's Liberation movement or any liberation movement instructs us, and although at an intuitive level I think it is clear, I believe I can make it clearer. Any liberation movement, by its very existence, asks two questions of all the people who are involved in its suppression. If you cannot avoid coming in contact with a Women's Liberation movement, then you cannot avoid dealing with those two questions which are basically the same questions for all liberation movements. The first is in the form of a statement — "You are a male chauvinist" — which you must answer either yes or no. There are many ways of answering no, such as the one I described at the beginning of the chapter. All of these ways turn out to be complicated methods of denying you are a male chauvinist — a male oppressor — an oppressor — part of the oppressing class and classes. And after all, who in his right mind wants to be part of the oppressing classes? But even if you manage to answer no to the question in one or another way, you are still not done with it, because by the very nature of such a movement existing in the society, it has a way of asking the question, making that accusation, over and over again.

However, if you should for some reason take the bit in your teeth and answer, "Yes, I do recognize that I am a chauvinist and therefore have allegiance to the oppressing classes," then you will get a chance to deal with the second question which is, "Will you continue to be part of this oppression?" Both of these questions ask us to make very fundamental judgments and choices about our lives, which we are asked to do in almost no other way. Because we are almost never forced to look at our involvement in oppression, and it is only when we are forced to look dead straight at it that we get the rare chance to say "No — no more." But if you say, "No, I will no longer conspire in your oppression," you have got yourself into a situation where you have committed yourself to escape from your class identity as a male oppressor. But that obviously leaves open the question of how you are going to make good the escape, where you are going to escape to, and who, if anybody, is going to hide you from the posse.

The metaphor of Women's Liberation gives an answer to that problem because it shows how women, when they began to feel wretched with their old identities in the society and the movement, had to reach down to the roots of their own oppression (stop trying to deal with their problems around the oppression of others) and create a liberation movement of their own.

The reason I say the only "successful" answer lies in accepting the metaphor that Women's Liberation gives is because I have seen the impotence and sickness and essential racism of liberal groups trying to appease their guilt about what they have done to black people. And although black people may be able to exploit that sickness in several ways, they will understand, and we must understand, that the guilt-stricken people they exploit are still racists and therefore still, at some very important level, their enemies. And the same applies to men and women.

And again, reasoning similar to this has led some men and some women to conclude that there should be a male liberation movement, but I am uneasy about this idea because I do not believe that men are oppressed on the basis of sex. Sex *qua* sex is not the basis of the oppression of men any more than whiteness *qua* whiteness is the basis of the oppression of Caucasians. Whites are used by the system through their racism and in that sense are oppressed by it, but that is not the basis of their oppression; it is the basis of black people's oppression. Similarly, men are used by the system in their role as chauvinists, but it is not the basis of their oppression; that lies somewhere else. And the directions to somewhere else must be made out of ourselves if they are to be made at all.

So all of this is very complicated instruction that comes to me from looking at the Women's Liberation movement and to a lesser extent at the black liberation movement and other liberation movements I have had even more remote contact with. What it has to do with love is that it points me to myself in a very challenging way that makes me feel the need, and feel the power of the need, for my own liberation. And the clarity I have about that need makes me more hopeful that I will find a stronger sense of myself that is not grounded in the need to keep somebody else down; that is more capable of love. And in a situation where I am involved in my own liberation, it is inconceivable that I would expect to find a relationship of integrity or love with a woman or a person who was not similarly involved.

Also, I like Women's Liberation because it is very shrewd, as a movement, in saying many things that make a great deal of sense to many kinds of Americans about America. It can teach people to see a great deal that they have not really seen before. And it is for this reason that I like the separatist wing of the Women's Liberation movement more than others, because it is more concerned with (confident of the validity of) portraying experience very vividly and acknowledging it as the primary teacher. Whereas I find women who keep translating their experience into existing political metaphors much less vivid and challenging and easier to dismiss, since they are using a language I already know and have already learned to use thoughtlessly and defensively/aggressively.

Finally, I like Women's Liberation because of what it has to say about love. Because many women in the Women's Liberation movement understand the reality of love as an issue in their lives and for their movement. Women talk about the need to be whole. And as their movement begins to grind down some of the distrust and competitiveness the society dictates women have for one another in their pursuit of men, women talk about, in very concrete ways, a real increase in their capacity to express love for one another. And that to me is a very hopeful sign.

Part 4

Images of the Future

14

Toward a Revolutionary Separatist Church and the Great Council of Revolutionary Separatist Movements

It is traditional for people of my cultural and political upbringing to conclude meetings and conferences and writings with a concise summary of things to do or projects to undertake, a plan of action sometimes called a tactic and sometimes called a strategy. And a long time ago, when I had formative ideas about this book, I'm certain I had a section of this sort in mind. However, whatever my original ideas were, they've pretty much slipped away, and I find that part of me feels that I should break with tradition and omit this section entirely.

But here it is anyway, because a commitment is a commitment and because I still do have this reflex in me that says it is

highly immoral not to include some organizational scheme.
Perhaps people who don't feel that obligation should ignore it
until they do, because once got, it is not easily got rid of.
People who do have it should understand that I write this
schematic and formal section primarily because I think the
organizational and strategic images we have at this time are just
basically wrong, not because I expect to open shop next week
with an operational version of what I talk about here. Or to say
this another way, I have come to feel that the real revolutionary
conspiracy in this country is *not* happening inside any of the
organizations that haul down the headlines or cling to the revolutionary labels. But it is happening. And it is happening as a
good conspiracy should, in twos and threes, among small groups
of intimate friends who engage regularly in the most rigorous
and intense ideological debates, even though the discussions
are most frequently called "talking to one another." I feel
strongly that the organized movement has not been able to
encompass or even touch large, deep, very committed segments
of revolutionary sentiment. And it is this feeling that leads me
to believe, on occasion, that we should just let go of all those
organizational images we have, because we can see, or at least
I begin to see, all the ways they have prevented us from growing, all the blind alleys they have led us into.

But it is only on some days that I feel this way. On other
days, most days, I know that despite the enormous mistakes we
inevitably build into our organizational schemes, we somehow
grow through them, we somehow have gotten stronger, not
just in spite of them, but because of them. Learning, at least
when it is this primitive, always goes three steps backwards in
order to take one step forward. But it turns out that one step
in the right direction is worth many more than three in the
wrong. So I will not give up my organizational insistence, even
though I criticize organizational efforts until my teeth grind
and my fingers ache, even though I sense that some of my
friends who have lost their organizational commitment have

grown beyond me and away from me in a very powerful way. In spite of everything, most of the political organizers I have been involved in has provided a way for me and others to grow and a way for us to learn, and it is important not to forget that or repudiate what was once true, even if we have grown beyond it. Even if we repudiate all of our old class and social identity and see that everything we have done and are doing now is hooked up to that old identity, we still must affirm the essential truth that underlies any human experience. We must remember that no matter how twisted they are and how many times they have nearly broken, all those organizations we have built are the truth we have grown by.

Still, the way I think about organization has changed a great deal. Before I got deeply involved in the movement, perhaps until the time I worked in the Cleveland ERAP project, I thought of political organizations in fairly standard ways — as sets of policies and chapters and officers and debates and public images and styles and rules of order and resolutions. I also thought of them as other things too — like friends and fun and good people and shared feeling and shared recognition. But this second set of things was somehow incidental — the fringe benefit, the pleasant but not really very basic part of the organization. The Real Organization in my mind was the first set of things, the organizational grist that churned out the organizational products — membership cards, newsletters, recruits, actions, publicity.

My involvement in SDS and particularly my experience in Cleveland, where we lived communally and really shared hardship and joy, gradually led me to see that the two sets of ideas were critically integrated. I realized that the whole quality of an organization rested on and grew out of what it did for the people who were in it in very concrete but ordinary ways like friendship and shared recognition. Gradually I integrated my ideas into a new image of organization that was much more organic. But I still felt, quite strongly as I recall, that the primary purpose of an organization had to be located outside of it, that it still could only exist legitimately if it was striving for some *external* goal. I still felt if an organization existed only for the people in it, then it was somehow just a therapy group or a social club, that it was somehow basically illegitimate. My sense was that the internal and external orientations of the organization had to *balance*, that we had to provide good enough lives for ourselves so that we could keep struggling to achieve the set of external goals called "organizing the community." It almost boiled down to needing to have a home to come home to at night after a hard day's work in the community — which if you think about it, doesn't sound so revolutionary.

These days I cannot conceive of being in an organization (ideological project) where internal and external are so easily distinguished. Or stated positively, the goals of an organization I would want to be part of would have to be goals that I could see as having flowed from or originated inside me and the other people in the organization; I would have to feel that the goals of the organization were about us, the people in it, not something or somebody else.

Organization in this new sense is the recognition of a certain kind of need we have to create a common fate. Organization is a bond and a pact, a charter of trust, a set of names and a kind of language, a place to live and a kind of life, and a way to know other people. Organization is a way of taking a set of ideas that we now have at the back of our heads and making it alive and vivid and real and connected to us. But since our ability to create language and life is so limited, and our capacity for trust so fragmentary, our organizations will have our scars stamped on them, and they will inevitably be collective representations of our failures and limitations. But they will, if we are lucky, also be mirrors of all of these things, alienated architecture that is nonetheless close enough to us so we can begin to comprehend the architect.

If these images correspond to any former image I have in my mind, it is not that of a political party or a "radical organization," or a club or a friendship group. But it is very definitely that of a church. Not of any church I have directly known or experienced, but of the church I have heard some churchmen talk about, the early revolutionary church, whose followers lived in caves and shared their bread, their persecution and their destiny.

I say church because in spite of what we observe them actually doing, churches stand for the salvation of men's souls, the salvation of the humanity (frequently called Godliness) of its members. I say church because church stands for a belief in a radically different, spiritually liberated life which is thought to be so changed as to be unimaginable to people who live in this world. I say church because church stands for communion, and it is the church feeling of communion that I believe must be at the bottom of any organization we build.

But of course I do not think these thoughts without being reprimanded by a voice that says, "You will get lost in all this religion stuff, it is a flight from reason and responsibility and knowledge — worse yet, it is a lack of confidence in yourself." Of course I know that there are no priests for this church and that even if there were, no one is to be trusted. But another part of me knows that there *is* love and someone *must* be trusted. So I seek a trustworthy man when I know there is none. And I seek to be a novitiate into a priesthood that I know does not exist.

It is obvious, of course, that there is no revolutionary church. The organized churches have given up on life — indeed seem to have been born out of a deep pessimism about living. They have forgotten or failed to see the revolutionary potential in people that made life worth hanging onto and have turned instead to selling defeated people various forms of funeral insurance. Except, of course, the modern churches, with all their secular wisdom, which have given up on death too.

We need a revolutionary church that is connected to our lives, that projects a vivid image of our capacity to love, that strengthens our belief in the reality of that capacity by teaching us to recognize and resist the oppression that has damaged it. We need a church that will separate us from our old class-based identities, that will help us validate our experience, that will make it possible for us to see that our oppression and our potential for liberation are shared. A revolutionary church must commit its members to their potential by embodying as much of it as it can, but it must also comprehend its own limits and struggle against them under the eye of its own vision. The strength of a revolutionary church would be in the reality of its separatism, the extent to which it was actually able to break people away from dehumanized life, the extent to which it could give them tools and concepts to live by, the extent to which it could make its vision concrete — provide substance for people to use. But its strength would lie equally in its recognition of what prevented the breakaway from being complete, in its ability to identify remaining limits and the weapons that could be used to attack them.

I realize that all of this is abstract — which is one of the reasons I hesitated to include this section. Perhaps a more modest statement would describe more adequately what I mean. Increasingly I am attracted to religious *images* like love and communion and soul and spiritual and church, even though my actual observation of the ways those words are used in organized churches has usually disgusted me. The corollary of this is that I am less impressed with hard political words like strategy and tactics and organize and struggle and action than I once was. Although I should make it clear that when I say "revolutionary separatist church" I have in mind some merging of revolutionary religious and revolutionary political ideas; I think of a strong, loving band of disciplined (but that is not the right word) people who are enabled by the spiritual solidarity of their community (communion) to explore and survive in the catacombs and caves of Western civilization and still maintain the faith.

Understood as a critique, what I am saying is that the movement has failed to make contact with the people who are in it, has failed to comprehend itself. The brittle, mechanical, alien nature of its language is a direct reflection of that incomprehension. Let me give one concrete example of the kind of distinction I am talking about as at least a partial apology for all these images and rhetoric.

Within the white, middle-class radical movement, it is very fashionable these days to talk about the need for "self-defense," so people learn karate or how to shoot guns, learn how to make explosives and practice machismo by threatening to beat one another up at sectarian political gatherings. But it seems all wrong to me. Not because I don't believe in the importance of self-defense or believe that a revolutionary church would be unconcerned with self-defense, but rather because I attach enough importance to the concept of self-defense (defense of self) that I cannot reconcile myself to seeing it caricatured by the movement. True self-defense begins only when people know enough about self to understand what is in danger, why it is in danger, and how it can be defended. For middle-class people, the instinct of self-preservation and self-defense is so deeply buried and distorted that it is extraordinarily difficult to put people in touch with it. It is much easier to tell their minds that the political line now includes self-defense and tell their bodies to jerk through a groin kick than it is to make them confront the fact that they are in trouble or under attack and explain to them why. Our minds are our most vulnerable spot. Our souls are a culturally repudiated potential. It is not a groin block we must learn; it is a head block. But the current system of teaching self-defense in the movement internalizes the destruction of the mind, becomes a kind of doublethink in which people are taught to swallow themselves in the name of defending themselves. It is very tricky, but this is how it happens.

The movement studies self-defense because "Repression is just around the corner," or because people believe that now is the time to begin to implement more militant, revolutionary tactics. But to tell someone that repression is just around the corner is to suggest to them that it is not now and has not been always and may not even be tomorrow. What is it a student experiences in a classroom? Liberation? Freedom? Identity? Repression in the mind of the movement is a physical act. It is a tightening of the reins on our constitutional privileges, it is a kid getting kicked in the groin by a cop. It is not a kid getting kicked in the head every day by a teacher. Self-defense is not learning how and when to stand up to the teacher or run from him or destroy him. It is preparation for something that has not happened or is not happening very much. And it is implicitly a denial of the validity of the other kind of self-defense. It is explicitly the process of externalizing a concept, of learning a rote reflex that has been imported from another culture.

Our first job is to explore all the ways we are being attacked every day in school, at home, on the job — in the places where we really live and are really hurt. We will recognize that attack only through a clearer recognition of ourselves. Our second task is to learn how to protect ourselves and how to begin to fight back. If we are ever able to do these two things, I suspect there will be no additional need to explain to people why they might have to learn how to defend themselves against a cop.

We need an organic, morally informed, conception of ourselves. That will tell us most of what we need to know about self-defense. The movement does not have this, and with its images of organization and politics, it is not about to develop it. That is why I find myself looking for a new image of or-

ganization. That is why I have begun to think about the need
for a revolutionary church.

The kind of church I have in mind can only be built around
a coherent group, a group that is defined by common class or
social experience. But to recognize this need for coherence, the
necessity of separatism, obviously raises some problems — particularly for radicals. The language of separatism is threatening. It is the harsh, didactic language of people who are
wrenching themselves loose from subservience, and radicals
have been afraid of it — for good reason. The radical vision is
built around the recognition that men are kept down by being
kept apart and the immediate consequence of separatism is to
exacerbate apartness, to make people understand all the ways
they are separate from and antagonistic toward other groups
in the society. It is one thing for black people to ask for ad-
mission into our society. We can tolerate that. Indeed, it is
very reassuring to know that other people value what we've
got. It reassures us we have something worthwhile. But it is
another thing for blacks to say, "Let me out; I want nothing
to do with you or any of the things you have to do with." That
is much too direct. It strikes at the root of too many problems
that have to do with why we are what we are. And it is the
worst offense for a woman to say it to a man. We are afraid
of separatism because it so drastically devalues us, because of
the awful fear we all have at some level that we will be left
alone in our misery, cut off from the supply of crumbs that
keeps us going, that makes life "meaningful." And at a social
level it speaks to our sense of fragmentation and impotence; the
sense, conscious or intuitive, that people are too far apart, too
intuitively out of tune with one another ever to accomplish any
real change in the world — the "knowledge" we have that
struggle is useless. And it is this kind of prior knowledge about
separatism that makes it such an anathema to radical political

people, because those people know better than most how an elaborate class and status system is used to keep people apart.

But we must face up to it. The fact of our lives is not the eventual creation of two homogenized and warring classes, as Marx so hopefully projected. The fact of our lives is constantly increasing stratification and separation, and despite my churchy orientation, I do not believe that you can make that fact go away by praying for it or trying ritually to exorcise it by adopting something called a "working-class line." It will not work. The thing must be turned loose. If social fragmentation is to be got out of, we must give up our search for an easy way. To get out, we must go through. If there are connections to be made with other oppressed groups, they must be made on the other side when we have finally broken or are well on our way to breaking our identities loose from the system. A revolutionary separatist church is not built to create a coalition with any other group; it is built to explore and resist the oppression of one group.

All this means that specific heresies must be allowed to occur. White women (not to mention black women) must be allowed to consider the possibility that black men oppress them (just as black men had to deal with the ways in which white women oppress them). Middle-class men must be allowed to understand the ways they are oppressed by working-class men. And if these examples increase the possibility for the expression of racism and class chauvinism, so be it; that is the direction we must go. Because if black men (just like white men) look at women as sexual objects — and they do — then for a woman not to react to that chauvinism in a black just as intensely as she does in a white in the name of an alliance, is to deny the reality and importance of her oppression, is to instruct her not to take herself seriously. And if radical middle-class men are not allowed to deal with or recognize their anger at the way working-class men use masculinity and machismo to oppress them, they create a movement that will lock part of their oppression inside and that will appear frantic and incomprehensible to most of the people it should have been addressed to.

The distinction I am trying to draw here is difficult. Because it should be intuitively clear that the image middle-class men have of working-class men does not correspond to reality. The contact between middle-class men and working-class men is too brief and tense, the society having designed it to be that way. Communication is structurally impossible. So the attempt seems doomed to ally itself with class bias. Similarly, the just feeling that a woman has about a black man objectifying her is not easily segregated from her racism — both themes having been so intricately intertwined. But the way out is not to hold it back. The way out is to put it out front where it conceivably might be dealt with.

But if we must actually heighten and sharpen the antagonisms that already exist among groups, how can we ever hope to create the possibility of collaboration? How can there ever be a Great Council of Revolutionary Separatist Movements? How could the "antimasculine" separatism I would be part of ever hope to reach rapport with a hypermasculine black separatism? Or better yet, how could black separatism work with women's separatism when Negro integration ran so directly amuck of women in the white integration movement? However, if you think about this question, it seems clear that blacks can only begin to have serious alliances with whites when they know that black people are fully in control of their own movement, when they understand that their movement *cannot* be controlled or compromised by whites, when the essential identity and direction of their struggle is their own. Furthermore, blacks could never work in a relationship of trust with whites whose motives are not clear — that is, whites who can still be suspected of *wanting* to control or manipulate their movement. But I believe it might be possible for black men to work with a Women's Liberation movement that was in no way con-

tingent on them for its definition — but in fact, like them, had
to maintain complete control of itself and its identity, could
accept no threat to its autonomy.

I am not saying it would be easy. I am not saying it would
not be proceeded by a good deal of screaming and shouting
about who really oppressed who. But I do believe that if you
are in touch with yourself, if you are confident that you know
your own need and know that nobody can take that knowledge away from you or manipulate it, then it is possible to
recognize other people who are in touch with their need. And
it is this intuitive recognition that might provide the motivation
and the bridge that conflicting separatisms could meet on.

Or to put it another way, the only way I can tolerate the
accusation of a black man that I am a racist is if I can disentangle myself from my racism. And the only way I have
been able to imagine doing that is to find an authentic identity
that is strong enough and clear enough to stand up without the
props of racism, chauvinism and class arrogance. It seems to me
that it is only in that situation that I could respond honestly
and clearly to his anger *without* betraying myself (and sub-
sequently hating him for having forced me to misrepresent
my emotions). And the same must be true for him in relation
to me. The possibility for integrity in a relationship is not
based so much on mutual admiration or even liking as it is on
the self-respect of each of the members of the relationship. If
we are in touch with ourselves, we will not be afraid of getting
lost or being humiliated. We will be able to sort out what is
said to us even if it is said angrily, even if not all the anger is
really applicable. And we will recognize in each other the trust
we have in ourselves — and we will learn to trust that too.
Implicit in the notion of separatism is a way to get beyond it.

And we do need to get beyond it. I do not believe that a just
revolution can proceed on the backs of any one group or social
class. The repression of all groups is so thorough that no one
group can possibly shake all of its allegiances to the past. But

liberation movements will be forced by necessity and enabled by shared self-recognition to create alliances of integrity and respect. And it is only when all the unique oppressions of different groups that have separated them from themselves and each other have come to a common recognition of a common necessity and a common need, that we can hope for a just revolution. It is the last contradiction in this book that I will ask you to embrace. It is only when we have finally reunited ourselves through separating ourselves that we will finally understand what an American revolution is all about.

Beyond the revolutionary separatist church, beyond separatism, is the Great Council of Revolutionary Separatist Movements. If you will, imagine for a moment a day when people representing each of the many ways in which we have been broken and internally fragmented, torn apart from each other and ourselves, can at last meet, look each other directly in the eye, find it in themselves to smile, and reach out. . . .

15

The Pressure for Definition

We are on the threshold of something new. That is a growing conviction in me, and it is confirmed not by the logic of what I write but by the fact that as I talk to people around the country I find more and more who in different ways express recognition of the same threshold. It is not that any *one* has the definition. No *one* can have it. It is that many find their thoughts being turned (forced) in the same direction.

More and more people begin to talk about the lack of authentic identity (authentic definition). But their talk is not the parlor-room talk of people who experience pointless frustration. It is not the never-to-be-answered "Who am I?" that

Freud's disciples have taught us to intone endlessly as a token of our own abasement. It is rather people saying first to themselves and then to others, "What is this thing that engulfs me, that propels me, that soaks up all my energy until I want desperately for it to let me go — but that keeps pushing me on? What has swallowed me and my friends? What is this pit we have fallen into? Who are *we?*" And the question brings back an echo, strikes a resonance in other people.

Who are *we?* It is a question that has an energy of its own. Part of the energy and insistence of the question makes me uneasy. I fear that one day I will whisper it and someone will shout back an answer and force me to deal with it. And I am not sure that I am ready for an answer, even though I sense that the answer is already in me and everybody around me but waits and waits and waits because we have not yet been forced to find the courage to listen to our own sentence, to grasp our own destiny. But the question will not now wait for us to answer it. It will make us answer to it.

People are beginning to see beyond the edges of their own amorphousness. Amorphousness is the feeling people experience when they struggle without definition. The movement is full of activity, but all of it is without adequate definition. For a while the war provided definition — purpose, a reason to struggle, a simple, unambiguous definition of what it was all about. Before that civil rights had provided definition. And most recently, the demand of blacks for recognition in the university has given definition. But all these definitions break down because they are external, and people again experience the amorphousness of no definition. In part, this explains the popularity of current sectarian styles and parties. They play at rigid clarity and they recruit people who must have it even if it means swallowing themselves.

To experience the amorphousness of the movement is to try to do something without knowing why. Or, as was the case with ERAP, to start doing something thinking you know why, only to find that the explanation can't hold the weight of reality — yours or theirs.

When I say people have begun to see beyond the edges of their own amorphousness, I mean that we have begun to understand that there is a force pushing the fog that surrounds us. We may not know what that force is, but we do understand it as the reason we keep attempting to *do* things. And the reason is not so much a logic as it is a perception that we have slipped into a stream, have been pulled gently into a current that is moving us even if we don't fully grasp it. We have gained a certain humility with that insight. We have learned that the world is bigger than our own logic. And as we have understood that, we have begun to stop thrashing so wildly against the current, have even begun to feel that we are part of the current.

We can begin to see that the thing we call a movement is not defined by a set of projects, insurrections and events. It is not a shopping list of activities that people around the country have thought up to do. All of those things are part of another thing, are encompassed by it, pushed ahead by it, dragged under by it, but always, methodically, moved by it. We are part of a social force.

One way of thinking about the activities we undertake is that they are attempts at definition. But none is adequate — largely because they define the universe with too narrow a logic. Nonetheless, while they last, they are important. They give people things to do and a partial rationalization for why they are being done. They keep us from going back or going crazy by keeping us busy, keeping our hands occupied. It makes sense that now, at a time when all projects seem to break down either in the direction of amorphousness or rigid sectarianism, many people begin to grasp that the movement in some very fundamental way is no longer describable as or even dependent on a set of activity. Rather it has become a social force, a cleavage in America, and tens of thousands of young people are discovering that they are on one side of that cleavage, swept up in the force that created it, without an adequate definition of that force (and themselves) and with less and less chance each day that goes by of getting back to the other side of the cleavage. But the new consciousness erases the old mystification of projects without filling up the time. How can you continue to do what you were doing once you recognize its essential make-work character? The result of amorphousness, of empty time, is that people are being forced out of projects and well-defined niches and up against themselves and each other — without a sense of direction, with only an ache for definition and a sense of motion and turbulence.

More and more people who are on the edge of the movement, who are potential recruits to it, who participate in some of its activities, are aware of the inadequacy of its definition for them, find that despite their attraction to it, there is nothing in it that speaks to their need. Eventually they find themselves in an equally imprecise, though perhaps more honest, thing called the youth culture. Both the dropout culture and the movement must be understood in the end as part of the same social force. But they do not define it.

In the current situation, the pressure for definition is enormous. Each day more and more people are dislocated, consciously or unconsciously, broken loose from their old feelings that they could get by in America, jarred or eased or jolted or floated into a new self-recognition that where things used to look okay and possible, now something starts feeling terribly wrong.

Each day there are new engineering students who find they can't concentrate on calculus. Each day more young women wonder how they could ever be housewives, more housewives remember something they once felt very strongly. Each day more kids look up at their teachers with total incomprehension; and each day a few more kids understand for the first time what this school business is really all about.

And as new people are dislocated, others find it even more inconceivable that they could ever be part of this country's design for them, begin to feel that there is no turning back, begin to realize that they know too much now to ever be able to successfully forget what they have learned, realize that they are committed by their knowledge to live in a new land. And this sense we have of being part of a social force also gives us the sense that there is a road to this new land and that we are on it or are at least looking for it. And there are all sorts of hawkers along the way shouting, "This way to the new land. This way to the new land." And either we've bought their stuff before and know that it is no good, or we begin to notice that as the hawkers scream they keep running alongside of us, trying to make us understand, trying to reach us, trying to keep up so they can keep shouting at us — being pulled along by the force that is pushing us in spite of themselves.

And as this social force grows in volume and intensity, it begins to come right smack up against itself on the one hand and the reality of the society's reaction to it on the other. Young people are beginning to realize that they are no longer the children of a "privileged" class, but are instead the hated, feared minority that the mainstream society describes and increasingly treats as vermin. And in the cross fire of these pressures from the society and each other's inability to sustain definition, there is more and more need to create a revolutionary, separatist, self-definition of ourselves. There is less and less chance to escape dealing with the question of who we are. It is when the last of the old self-definitions has collapsed and the only place left to look for self-definition is to one another that we will realize who we are, remember the thing we forgot so long ago, be able to announce in our own name that we are part of the revolution in America.

16

Images of the Future

The Morality of Beer Cans

How easily they sell us all that progress junk. I remember when they first came out with the flip-top beer and soda opener, I was pissed and angry. I thought to myself — and probably told a number of people with a good deal of self-satisfaction at my insight — now this is what America is really all about. Some highly trained engineer or set of engineers spend five years experimenting with different ways of stamping metal until they come up with a gismo like this, patent it, and then one by one coerce beer companies into paying the extra price so their beer can will be as "modern" and "convenient" as any on the market. So incrementally the price of beer and other things goes up (I mean the real price as measured in the amount of human energy and resources that goes into making something), all for the sake of getting something nobody really needed. As a matter of fact, not only didn't need, but didn't want — or at least my recollection is that it was always kind of fun to open a beer can without squirting the damn thing all over everyone and about as inconvenient as stretching.

But then today, just a few years later, I went to the refrigerator for a bottle of soda, reached down to pull the ring top, only to discover it wasn't there, having, as they do occasionally, broken off. I was immediately pissed and irritated. Something that I'd come to expect to happen (nothing more) had been interrupted, and as a result I was upset. Somehow, ring-top cans had become the right way to do things and a can without a ring-top was almost morally wrong. And this is a device I had been consciously aware of having objected to. How many other things are foisted on us all the time without our even being aware of it, and yet become components of our moral environment by virtue of their very pervasiveness?

I can almost see myself tottering on the front porch swing, telling an incredulous grandson how it was in the olden days when people used to use can openers. I mean, how would you justify a can opener to someone who had grown up all his life without them. It's almost inconceivable.

Hanging onto Winter

It has been a hard winter; but now it is ending and I think I will miss it. The days are already part of spring, but there is so much snow on the ground that they cannot reach it — and so the illusion of winter hangs on. While it was here, it consumed me; there was no time to reflect on it, being here with so few resources — not enough fuel, not enough money, no friends near at hand. It spent my energy trying to survive it. It is only now that it is going that I observe it — understand for the first time that the leafless, barren tangle which at this very moment is beginning to live again, is a more honest (more compatible) description of what exists here than the rush of color that will overtake the sky and groundscape in a few weeks.

That color will mask what is now so easy to see — the bare, unattractive outlines of the houses, the thicket of undergrowth that confronts you everywhere you move — brittle, confusing twigs that claw your face and snag your pant legs — the residue of two hundred fifty years of Western civilization, the twisted wreckage of what once was a forest. It is not that there is not beauty in this place. It is rather that the beauty is the beauty of wreckage — the beauty of decay, and the skeletal, stringy life that grows out of it. It is too easy to be confused in the springtime and think that you have found the wilderness. The color is nature's appeasement to man's carnage — or a declaration that if only man would stand aside, a forest could be made to grow out of all this brush.

Perhaps we must learn to cherish the cold, twisted outlines of wreckage, to learn that life is a struggle for survival with real devastation, not to contemplate the spring that will come to cover it with color, but to try to imagine what it was like when this was wilderness, to try to think what it would be like once again to put things in harmony with one another.

The Last Part

It is important to think about the potential for human evolution because that is one of the ways of thinking about human nature, and most of this book has been an attempt for me to illustrate with the metaphors that my life has given me what I think our nature is as human beings and how I think it is that our nature has been defiled. So that when I say think about human evolution, I mean think about what we would be like if we were no longer defiled, think about the highest expression of our potential we can conceive. Of course that implies I do not think our potential is infinite, which I do not, although I know one of the ideas I grew up believing, and one of the ideas most of us grew up believing, was in the "infinite perfectability of man's infinite capacity." But that idea was very hooked up with the progress machine — with this whole sense of Western history that said that despite all evidence to the contrary, man was really being liberated by technology, and technology and science were limitless frontiers. So we have always imagined utopia as a setting, as a certain kind of place that is always populated by people and their machines and the dwellings for both. And furthermore, we all did grow up with some sense of utopia — that is, with the sense that ahead of mankind lay a much better future, dominated by machines and people. Of course you will say that is a very natural way to think, which it is for people growing up in this era, living in the West or perhaps anywhere; but in fact there is no logical reason why people should not think of utopia as being dominated by animals or vegetation or colors or sounds or some combination of those things. But in fact, what we grow up with, at least until the time we begin conscious rebellion and probably for most people even after that point, is a sense of utopia that is full of machinery and structures. And we do have this sense of utopia, because the society very definitely projects these images of itself into the future.

How could the future be any different when we have this overpowering sense that history, human evolution to this time, has been the story of technological evolution? There is almost no other way to think about it. You have to go back to the cavemen with their very primitive technology and the unelaborate, subsistence culture that implied, and then watch it all unfold till world history books invented the wheel and General Motors invented the car and John Kennedy invented the clean bomb. So there it is, just as straight as any road can be, taking off right out of the primeval ooze and going on right up to the present and then over the hill into the future and then on and on and on forever with this incredible record that anybody who wandered from the road or couldn't keep up invariably and without exception got wiped out.

So it must sound like the most extraordinary understatement to say that technology has played an important part in human evolution and no more, but that is all that I am willing to say — just that it has been important — nothing more. Because history really does depend on who's writing it, and it's clear that our whole sense of history, written and unwritten, has been made by people who were all wrapped up in these positivist ideas about the ascendance of our technology, and who were obviously not very interested in finding evidence that suggested they weren't on the main track of history. Even revolutionaries couldn't set aside that conceit. One thing they always granted to the old society that they were challenging was that it was on the right track even if it had chosen the wrong form. So to extend the metaphor just a little bit longer, it's as if everybody, all the good guys and all the bad guys, have collaborated in putting up signposts that all point to the same road and warnings that say all other roads lead to the great junk heap of history.

But if you look at history, just a little bit deeper, you realize that the old road isn't altogether that straight — as a matter of fact, has some positively hairpin curves where it seems to completely double back on itself. At the most superficial level, think of all those technologically superior civilizations that just declined and decayed and died, even though they were the toughest thing going at the time — Egypt, Mesopotamia, Crete, the Incas, Rome. And the most interesting thing is not that those civilizations declined, because it's really easy to see in retrospect how barbarous each of them was in its own way, but the most interesting thing is that historians always think of the decline as mysterious, as somehow hidden from historical observation. Try as they may, they can never come up with an adequate explanation, because our whole big sense of history tells us that those civilizations should at least have lasted until some technologically superior civilization came along and toppled them. The explanations historians come up with, although they are very pale, usually concentrate on some internal stress in these civilizations, some class antagonism or some flaw in the fiber of the people, some softening (people soft, technology hard). They never seem to comprehend that perhaps it was the technological orientation all these civilizations shared that made those stresses, rather than as is assumed, some imperfect organization of that technology; or for that matter, that it was the technological orientation of those civilizations in the first place that made them interesting and semicomprehensible to historians who were trying to write their own history. It's something we're incapable of imagining; man fails, obviously, but technology never does.

But I feel very strongly that we must consider the possibility that technological organization and evolution, so far as human beings are capable of sustaining it, is reaching its limits — that is, the kind of culture humans can create that is susceptible to technological organization without completely shattering has been developed as far as it will go or pretty close to it, or perhaps even, already, further, and that we may have finally reached the junction, after a hundred thousand years or so, where the choice between human evolution continuing and technological evolution continuing will be decisive. And to think about that would mean of course to think about the possibility that our fathers and forefathers and we ourselves may have been off the main course of history, which for Americans, even radical Americans, is one of the hardest thoughts to entertain, since we all grew up with this strong feeling that we were at the center of the world and at the center of history even if we thought about that center in negative terms.

It is possible that a country like China or Vietnam that is having a revolution in this era yet still has not got our incredibly heavy technological equipment defining life for people, and which at the same time is surrounded by the extraordinarily clear examples of Western decadence and technological humiliation, that such a country would find a way to begin to reconstruct itself on other principles. Difficult as that is to believe, it is important to consider and realize that if such a thing were to happen and if such a culture were to become ascendant, as I think it would, then the whole story of human evolution would have to be drastically rewritten to try to explain why these aberrant and very destructive forms of culture grew up in the West, and also to discover the principles of life which we have completely lost track of, that were preserved in nascent form in some other part of the world despite all the wars of the West upon them.

It is even possible to consider that such a revolution would happen in the West as the technology machine shatters itself in its own destructiveness to human culture, that the principles of its antithesis would somehow be reborn out of the disintegration. And although these are images that we are unfamiliar with, I have a very strong feeling that they are images that have begun to grow again in our time.

But all of this is preliminary to saying that when I think about the evolution of human culture as opposed to the continued evolution of technology over man and the continued abasement of human culture, I begin by trying to dispense with the machinery and think about the creature. And that, it should be clear, means for me trying to think about whether there is any way to resolve this conflict — which I talked about in the very beginning of the book and have really just kept elaborating in different ways throughout — the conflict between what children, all children, see in alleys that societies repress, the conflict between me and others, the conflict between emotional vividness and social cogency, the conflict that destroys the possibility for authentic experience, the conflict that creates the need and destroys the possibility for love. And the amazing thing for me is that when I think of this paradox, I believe it could be overcome. Not in our lifetimes. Not in the lifetimes of anybody who is alive in the world today, because it is clear that all of us have got a consciousness that is basically defensive and that has permanently crippled us, but I find that I do believe that over generations, if human evolution were to begin to move in another direction, that paradox could end.

It is possible for me to imagine that as human culture began to loose the stranglehold that technology has on it, people would gradually begin to be repressed less — that in a society that did not dictate competitiveness and mammoth bureaucracy, and the massive, dull interaction of people who must be numbed to prevent them from interacting as people, children would actually grow up with less shattered senses of themselves — and therefore with less fear that people around them were going to deplete them — and because of that with more capacity to love, and because of that with greater ability to bring children into human culture without brutalizing them. If that image seems much too simple it is because we have never imagined what people would be like if the mandates of technical organization were not the principles for the socialization of people. Think what must be done to the animal to make a man willing to work in a factory all his life. Think what must be done to the animal to make people posture in front of each other as they do. Think what must be done to the animal to make it so terrified of life, so victimized by death. And if you think of our society as a great conspiracy to do these things and yet realize that the human animal has so far survived and even shows some resilience, you begin to realize what a terribly strong creature this human animal is and what it has endured without completely losing hope; and if you think about this strength, then perhaps you will understand why I imagine human evolution would be such a simple process once the grip of technology was broken.

But as I have said, I do not believe this process could happen so quickly, that is, in the lifetime of any one generation, although on the relative scale of all human history, it might happen quite quickly, say over a dozen or even fewer generations, which when seen from a future that no longer marks time out as another instrument of fragmenting our lives, or when seen as the last explosive act of labor in the unhappy, hundred-thousand-year birth of human potential, would not seem like very long at all.

It is hard, of course, to imagine what all this might look like, but there are nonetheless feelings I have, which I know I share with many people, that do describe a sense of it. And the fact that they are shared suggests that many people do have a common feeling about the area in which human potential lies, which is one more indication that that potential does have some seeds in this country.

Perhaps the most powerful element in that image is that the boundaries that currently separate us as "individuals" begin to melt until they are completely gone or only vaguely discernible, that all life lives in us with an emotional force stronger than any human alive could now endure, and that we live in all life, seeing with its eyes and feeling with all of its senses. In such a world, our memory would stretch back to the very beginning of life and forward to the return of this planet to the sun, the reunion of this planet with its birth in its death, in the process of making whole again the fragmented space of the universe. We would know these things not in some cognitive sector of our minds called imagination, but in our memories which themselves would be part of our present — because in such a world there would no longer be any need to forget. And perhaps as strong as any feeling I have is that the thing we call language would no longer occur; it would be too utterly inadequate to express relationships among people. If people made sounds our ears could discern, we would hear them as strange music that would be in harmony with the sound of birds and crickets or the noise of little children playing, but would have no connection in our recollection to what we call speech. And if we could watch people move against the background of their music, we would know at once that they were dancing — dancing with the rhythm of waves and with the pulse of tree limbs blowing under the wind.

But I know that some people will be revulsed by these images. Arthur Clarke, in *Childhood's End*, creates similar images out of similar insights (clouded by the phantasmagoria of science fiction), only to conclude that the creation is not human, but is something that is beyond pessimism and optimism. But I share little of that ambivalence. My individualism is a smelly sack I was thrown into as a little child that has always constrained my movements, filtered out the light, and suffused all smells in its smell. My personality, when I think about it most openly, is still defensive. And if I can never transcend that defensiveness, I can nonetheless recognize and be excited by an image of what life might be like without it. In the last analysis, this book does not have to rest on some grand theory of history and technology, but only on that common recognition, which is essentially intuitive, that this is what we could be and that it would be good.

But there are those who will say that these are pretty images but will refuse to consider them seriously because they do not believe we could do without our technology — see it, as I think it is popular to see it, as the simultaneous repressor and liberator of man, and therefore, as Marx understood it, the engine that must be harnessed, but oh so definitely the engine. Again, our upbringing makes such thoughts almost beyond contemplation. What would we ever do without the cars and the refrigerators and the tin cans and the doctors (most of all the doctors) and the mechanics and the masons and the sewer cleaners? And what about creation and science and the exploration of space and the discovery of the origins of the molecular change called life? And what about art and literature and all man's other noble creations?

But I believe a healthy human being would be bored by an automobile or a pyramid called a skyscraper, and although he might be delighted by a molecule, he would not have to see it to believe it was real. I believe that healthy human beings could learn to accept the delicate instructions their bodies gave them about what to eat and how to eat it and comprehend natural ecology enough to unwreck it and link themselves to it as sustainers and recipients of life. And in such a culture, health would not be an occupation of a high priesthood called doctors, but would be so intricately linked with all the emotional and physical aspects of living and all the lore of history as to be unthinkable as the domain of specialists. Nor would healthy human beings need magicians to protect them from their fear of· death or anesthetics to insulate them from the experience of pain. Nor would healthy human beings need to be entertained by TV or the Boston Red Sox. Nor by hi-fi — since the music that men made in harmony with their world would be so much richer and evocative. No, not even the Living Theatre, which would have faded into the memory of the time when men spent their lives on stages. And most remarkable of all, I even believe that healthy human beings could set aside their expressways, step out of their cars, and walk the great, greening earth again, and embark on great voyages spanning many years that would take them into unknown, distant lands.

Part 5

Postscript

Postscript

1

It is six months since I "finished" writing this book, and I am now involved in a final "editing" before it goes off to be immortalized in a binding. Many important feeling things have happened to me during this time and I want to try to talk about a few of them here — sort of because this is my last chance to set things straight before they turn to printed stone — but also because one of the most important things to happen to me since I stopped writing this book is that I have stopped thinking of myself as a writer or a person who is writing a book.

Actually, it's a little bit trickier than that. Because all the time I was writing the book, I kept telling myself I really wasn't a writer, but I kept telling other people when they asked me what I was "doing" that I was "writing-a-book," and I kept telling myself that the reason I was telling other people I was writing a book was because it was the kind of self-description I knew was pretty acceptable in the world of my friends — writing a book about politics, teaching a radical course, working on a movement paper, organizing a this or a that — these were all acceptable ways of describing what you were doing in my world. But actually, from fairly early on, I knew that writing the book was only a part of what I was doing. The other things, the things I didn't announce when someone asked me what I was up to, the things that increasingly became important, were things like trying to get my head together, trying to make a relationship with Leni (referred to elsewhere in this book as a friend) that had some integrity, trying to relearn how to live with myself, alone, in the country, trying to talk more honestly and engagingly to friends. And even though I knew this and even though I actually only spent somewhere around two days in seven "working on the book," I continued to describe myself as a person who was writing a book. And of course at some level the deception of my friends was self-deception because precisely to the extent that I felt I needed to (or found it simpler or more convenient or less tense to) project an image that I *thought* was more acceptable, I felt guilty and illegitimate about the other things I was doing (or its corollary — felt hemmed in and resentful toward my friends). And in this particular sense I was a writer throughout — a person who has emotional and ego investment in thinking of himself as a person who writes.

Anyway, it was all this stuff about being a writer in my head and in the world that stopped when I stopped writing the book last October (1969), typed it and sent it off to a publisher (who promptly rejected it). And the problem is that when I stopped being a writer, I began to discover how much of a prop that definition had been. I had painted myself into a corner, used the book and the time it had given me to work myself completely (or almost completely) out of the organized political movement but into nothing else, at least into nothing else defined in the old way — like a job. I was just a person alive in America who had written a book that probably wasn't going to get published and who couldn't think of "anything he wanted to do."

Not being a writer has meant a great deal to me and one of the things it has led to is a feeling that I understand quite clearly some of the major weaknesses of this book and can talk about them, even if I can't get particularly beyond them.

Not being a writer has helped me toward a reconstruction of my power fantasies. I really don't know quite how to talk about this because unlike a lot of the things in the book, I'm not sure I can talk about "our" power fantasies because I'm not sure how much mine are like everybody else's — since I've only begun to be able to *think* and occasionally talk about mine in the last half year.

I have always wanted power, but I have never been able to admit it, even to myself. I have always gotten power over others and in organizations by being pleasant, intelligent, self-effacing and noncompetitive. I always got other people to push me forward; I always accepted their pushes reluctantly, partly out of my elaborate false modesty, partly out of genuine fear about using power. The fear of using it was very much like the fear of seeking it or the fear of admitting I wanted it.

But writing a book, any kind of book I suspect, but particularly this book and this kind of book, involved me very deeply in my power fantasies because there was just no way for me not to daydream about what it would mean if the book was important and lots of people read it and felt moved by it. I felt the whole excitement about the media, having something printed, becoming well known or famous, being discussed in the ways people discuss books and authors and big men in general. But of course I couldn't really admit the importance of those fantasies, since I was into denying my desire for power and certainly into denying that I wanted "big man" status — you may recall my denunciation of it in the first chapter. So here I am six months later, reading the first chapter, realizing that my book departs from a kind of half-lie. And I *am* embarrassed to admit it. However, since one of the things I feel strongly these days is that we all lie a lot — all speak with forked tongues — except on rare occasions — I am less embarrassed than I might otherwise be. I say "half-lie" because there has been a conflict all along. Part of me fears the kind of power that part of me wants. People who make clear, ego-involved competitive attempts for power frequently get shot down, defeated, beaten, rejected. And I really don't want to be rejected. I want you to like me. So long as there is a discernible top and bottom, people who are on the top will always be justly feared and hated by people who are at the bottom. The perversion I fall into is wanting to be at the top while appearing to want to be at the bottom. The folklore image of Abe Lincoln is so lovable because it is about a man who was supposed to be genuinely simple and modest who made it to the top.

A way to say all of this that is a little less harsh to me is that part of me wanted a less alienating, less frightening kind of power. The problem with the book is that it presents "images" of me and the world and us rather than getting at the real hard conflicts I feel in myself, the hard to talk about, unre- solved, half-admitted conflicts that most affect the way I feel day to day. The book is not usually close enough to the edge of me; most of the things that are in it were too easy to say.

Not all of them however. Some parts were very hard com- ing and very hard to say when they did come, and it is those parts I like most and that I still feel closest to. Most of the stuff on love and sex was like that (even if it got pretty stylized in writing) and only a little of the rest was. But in the end, the book as a whole is too abstract and guarded and so am I.

2

I am less involved in changing America than I was when I wrote the book. This does not mean that I am any less angry or upset or horrified by this country than before. If anything, I am more profoundly and intuitively aware, day to day, of what an ugly society this is and how desperately it needs change. But my information about the country comes less and less from the papers — more and more from my own experience with it.

The only newspaper I read avidly is the (San Lorenzo) *Valley Press*, a weekly shopping newspaper delivered free to everyone in the Valley which, in an attempt at good old small town Americana, sandwiches local scandal and excitement (every arrest — even minor ones, but especially pot busts — robberies, misallocations of funds, articles on drug "abuse") between supermarket ads. There are also letters to the editor — people "letting off steam" — which give clues about what is going on in some of the minds in this community. It is a good paper from my point of view. It tells me a lot of what I want to know. It tells me more than the *New York Times* or the *San Francisco Chronicle* for example. It is less sophisticated and therefore less successful in smoothing over the craziness that is going on. Specifically it confirms that some substantial percentage of this community is fixated on me — although they call us "drug abuse."

But my real source of information is what I see. I meet people from the "straight" world who are afraid of me — because of the way I look. What they see is not simply long hair (each year I have less hair and what I have is long — but not all that long) or hippie garb (I wear pretty much the same nondescript clothes I've always worn, with the exception of a woven belt Leni made). There is something other than hair or clothes or stereotypes or postures that they see. I'm not sure what it is — perhaps a threat to the precarious stability of their own adjustment to the society — but whatever it is, it is a real threat and it evokes real fear.

I have seen women look at me in much the same way I have seen white women look at black men — look at me with some sort of mixture of fear and hostility and sexual attraction/ repulsion. I know that I am part of other people's paranoid fantasies — but I also know there are real reasons for that. Things are surfacing — in me and around me — that previously were pushed way down inside. Every trip to the store or the movies or the university or a party holds the potential of turning into a political encounter — a political demonstration.

But they are not political encounters that I in any way go out of my way to find — and that is important because it spells out the difference between a political *stance* and a political *life*. I am not "looking for trouble." Trouble is finding me. I do not need to go to Chicago or dress in some special way or *act* outlandish in the supermarket or a plastic restaurant or put anybody on or become an outlaw or a bomber or occupy anything other than my own life in order to confirm my suspicion that this is a brutal and dangerous country — in order to see the depth or breadth of the chasm that is opening. All I have to do is walk into the office of a sheet metal shop to get a piece of stove pipe made and see the secretary look at me like a plantation field hand. All I have to do is let one small piece of my anger and hostility out and watch my "therapy group" turn on me. All I have to do is go to the University of California at Santa Cruz and watch the students whipping themselves (and me) at a "political meeting." All I have to do is live my life. In fact, I don't even have to leave my house to know real danger. It is right here, in me, and in all my relationships with all the people around me. The objectification/recognition that was going on in Chicago is going on here. We have simply dispensed with the organizing committee and the TV cameras.

There is danger in the outside world. I feel it. And I don't believe my feeling is paranoid. I see looks in people's faces and I read things people say that assure me that my sense of danger has a foundation. And the danger is increasing. I believe this country is crazier than it has ever been before. Or perhaps I should say the craziness is more and more spilling out of the channels that were built to contain it.

But I also have a sense about the restraints that still hold the society's paranoia and anger in check. They are breaking down, but they have hardly shattered. They may have completely shattered for the Vietnamese and they may have almost completely shattered for black Americans, but they have not completely shattered for me. My most realistic fear about what this society might do to me directly and punitively at this point is unemployment or a pot bust. There is a chance that I could get harassed or terrorized by vigilantes or cops, but it is not happening very much in this area at this time. I do not have to direct all my energies toward physically defending myself from the world.

But it is right here that I have gotten in trouble in the past. I have felt guilty about the fact that I have space that the Vietnamese don't, and I have tried to cut down the distance between me and the Vietnamese by *making* confrontations with the society, trying to change it, or feeling bad about not doing those things. The effect is to throw away the space I have and perpetuate the guilt-stricken notion that I can escape from my life. But I can't. No one can — including the people we keep insisting have escaped — the people in the suburbs. But they didn't. They got killed — not by American napalm but by American "know-how." The only escape from life is death.

The problem with this book is it tries to escape into the

future. It is hopeful about the possibility of discovering class identity and of making some movement out of the merging of separatist consciousnesses. It perpetuates the "ought" — that we ought to work toward the emergence of a unified resistance to America through the development of certain ideas or forms. It suggests that there are still things that we have to make happen.

But my experience is exactly the opposite. The less I am involved in making things in the world (a movement, a book, an ideology) or making something of me (a stronger person, a crazier person, a revolutionary), the more happens. I have always been involved in trying to make my current situation into something else. I have always thought that I was trying to make something else because of some lack in me or the situation. But in fact, the only thing missing in the current situation is me. When you get right down to it, I do not fly to the Vietnamese cause out of guilt or identification. I fly to it out of fear — of my own life.

I am full of anger, energy, love, hatred, resentment, hostility, tranquillity, courage, fear, insight, blankness, futility, hope, desperation, panic, peace, power. All of that is happening. I do not have to make any of it, nor can I unmake any of it. I do not have to go anywhere to find it. It is here. I want to stop manufacturing my life and my politics. If there is a choice, it is that — to experience myself and my situation. But I'm not sure it *is* a choice. Rather, it makes more sense to say, it is what is happening.

Most of what I have tried to tell in this Postscript is what is happening to me. It may not sort itself out; it may not cohere; and it probably doesn't "lead anywhere." But it is as much of where I live these days as I can get on this paper.

3

I frequently feel withdrawn and alone and bad these days. I have real troubles relating to other people. I get very tight in social situations and frequently get tied up in fear of contact — averted eyes, avoided topics — trapped inside myself in a room full of people.

I want to get out. It makes sense to say that. I want to meet people openly and bravely. I feel much better when I do. I want to be able to affirm the connection between me and other people; I want to make it real. (See me making me again.) But it doesn't seem to happen. I am alone in almost all my enterprises — writing, cooking, getting wood, walking in and feeling this country, meditating, listening to music, making music, making fires, smoking dope, sleeping. Things that are shared are almost always shared with the same person — Leni. The vortex of my life is located at one primary relationship. I need to talk about that — work on what it means, find out what my friends think about it, try to reach all my feelings about it, understand what it has to do with my feelings of isolation.

There is a question about what my life is about now. There is so much uncertainty about how to live. I do not know how to relax in your presence.

Maybe this helps to get closer. The old focus, the old politics ("new politics") that carried me from fall 1957 through the first three months of 1970 is gone. The old focus helped me to be clear about certain things, gave me confidence in my anger, gave me a way to relate to other people, literally gave me a set of things to talk about (the war, the movement, capitalism, the destruction of the possibility of human community), gave me an arena that I felt comfortable in, made me feel less alienated and alone, gave me a way to reach out.

Now the old focus has gone — or at least has lost its sharpness. The old conversations and categories seem too abstract, the old reaching out somehow never got beyond a charismatic offer of something beautiful that I could not actually deliver with any one person or set of people, face to face. In its place, there are only impressions and fragments — except there is a relationship with Leni — focal and primary — a place where sometimes I can relax and share and reach out and find good things.

The problem I feel is something like how to get out a statement about all the ways I feel swallowed up into the world of Leni and me, all the ways in which I sense our (mine and Leni's) isolation and privateness and ingrownness — without getting into denigrating in myself the integrity of being at where I am at. Or, to say it another way, the most difficult thing to sort out is the difference between a real desire to be out of hiding and a sort of punitive, immobilizing shame and guilt about myself.

But in fact there is very little rising above the muck for me these days. There is primarily the feeling of going deeper — of getting into the mess that the language of the book implied I could get out of. I am less connected in my head to other people now than when I wrote the book. What impresses me most of the time is the frailty and insecurity of my relationships with other people. I see that we (me and the people around me) are in pretty serious trouble, that we cannot go on this way, but I can't say it. I can say it in here — relatively simply. We are in trouble — now. But I can't say it in a room full of my friends. I can't see "we." I can't identify us. What I feel is not that "we" are coming together, but that we are falling apart, falling away from one another — falling into isolation, hiding, prison. The book should help me make the identification and connection, but it doesn't. The immediate effect of living with fewer of the old prescriptions is seeing how much real distance between us they covered up. And part of my reaction to seeing that has been to retreat, to draw back, to become distant (literally far away from people). My sense is not particularly that the falling apart is near an end — which is another change from the book. The book is hopeful and visionary about how we are coming together. It never quite comes to grips with how fundamentally we are falling apart.

I do not particularly feel that the feelings I have now are ones that could be avoided. I realize I have felt them for a long time. It is now, however, that I find myself trapped in the same room with them. I do not want to fall into the book trap of implying that being here with these feelings is a better place to be than somewhere else. I do not want to say that everyone has to go through this. I have to go through it. (There is a problem even in saying this is something I am going *through*. It implies that I see a way to come out, but I'm not sure that I do.)

I'm not sure that "falling apart" is the right phrase. "Tearing apart" is probably better. We are already stuck together by all sorts of conventions which are quite general and pervasive in nature, but which lock us into historically specific freezes with everyone we know. So there are connections — the wrong connections — but nonetheless very important connections since they are the only ones I have — or perhaps I should say, the only connections I see. Leni and I see the ugly, stultifying, punitive, guilt-ridden connections — see all the ways we are "better" with people we are less deeply connected to, and feel torn up and apart by a lot of our fights. The tearing feeling is very literal; it feels like someone has been tearing at my guts or pounding on them.

The fights do not particularly make me feel like we are about to break up — although I am more frightened by what it would mean to "lose" Leni than I ever have been before. But the residues of the fights do not go away; I do not "get over" them. They do irreparable damage (irreparable good). They break things that before seemed unbroken; they tear away more.

I know that we are not supposed to be tearing each other apart. We are supposed to be building each other up, helping each other put together and connect well. We are supposed to be tearing apart the society that tore us apart originally — not one another. We are supposed to be tearing down the walls of the private "personal ghettoes" that Alta talks about. But instead we live in our insular, private shells and get more and more angrily distant from one another.

4

Maybe just one thought. I am not sure that I will ever do any approved revolutionary acts. It is possible that I will never be able to look right straight in the eye of the forces that compromise me, and spit. It may simply never happen. I am hardly convinced that my will is invincible. But it does seem to me that it is possible for me to be in touch with children. And that seems important. It is possible to think of having children without that being a form of "giving up." It is possible for me to recognize my life-sustaining other life and affirm it.

5

I just realized that one of the things that I have been doing during the last few days is getting up and walking out of rooms I didn't want to be in. I have done it a lot. I have walked out of situations (rooms) I could not deal with, and come back to them when I could — only to leave a few minutes later when things began to slip away. I have broken a literal paralysis — the one that says it is impolite to walk out on people (to reject them by leaving their presence). I have used my power of self-locomotion in somewhat the same way I see eighteen-month-old Kelsey using his. When Kelsey gets tired of something or doesn't want to or can't deal with it, he simply moves away. No one has taught him to sit still and be polite.

He also keeps the things he is afraid of under penetrating observation. He is afraid of dogs and he constantly wants to know more about them. He has not been taught to bury his fear or suppress his instinctual knowledge of survival. He has not yet learned how to run away from life. And hopefully he never will. There are a lot of things I feel he can help me with.

6

I want to try to clarify one of the things I said in the chapter on Women's Liberation and get deeper into the reality of my connection to women and that movement. I said I thought the women's movement was very shrewd in saying many things that made a great deal of sense to many Americans about America. What I meant was that I hear women talking about the experience of living in America — *their own* experience. I hear women talking about what it is like to work in a kitchen all your life. This is something I've always known — that women work in kitchens (and raise children and do housework), but I have known very little about what it felt like, what the real experience of working in a kitchen is. I did not know that even though I grew up in a family where men shared in the housework and where notions of this being unmasculine were talked about and pretty deeply and explicitly rejected. My father even took responsibility for certain household chores — vacuuming the rugs for example was something he pretty much always took care of without any coaching or organizing from my mother — something I realize in retrospect was fairly unheard of among my parents' friends and acquaintances. But even though I grew up feeling that housework was a reasonable activity for men to be involved in and even take some responsibility for, no one ever threatened to label me a "housewife." It was always clear — never in doubt for a moment — that I would never be asked to define myself or identify myself as a "housewife and mother" (houseworker and child-raiser). I could "share" in those responsibilities — even consider without much difficulty taking "equal" responsibility — but I would never be *defined* by them. It is totally unpermissible to think of rearing a boy child to be a housewife. My parents always knew and I always knew as everybody

knows — it is simply too degrading. It is an incredibly degrading definition for a man — because a man is supposed to
be something. I also knew that the world of jobs, politics,
prestige, status — the world of being — was pretty much a
world for men. Women could participate in it on a part-time
basis but their real definition, in my head, had to remain housewife and mother. A woman who did not have this definition
did not have a complete life. There is still part of me that
believes that. The training is very deep.

But I only begin to see all this and understand what it means
and has meant when women begin to talk about what it means
to be reared as a kitchen worker. The interesting thing is that
I had not seen earlier what I had so clearly "understood"; I
had not seen how awful it would be to be reared as a kitchen
worker or I had not applied my knowledge of that to women;
I had assumed that they would not feel as I do about being
kitchen workers; I had assumed that it was okay with them to
have a definition I would find terribly degrading — I have
ignored what they felt — until women made it impossible for
me to ignore it (them) anymore.

I mean all of this quite literally, because my most basic
weapon against women, I have realized recently, is to ignore
them. The way I put women down to this day is at some level
not to pay attention to their existence. When I actually see
myself doing it, I'm startled because I am usually unaware of
it. I find myself in a conversation with a woman, talking in-
telligently and clearly and "responsively" to what she is saying, and then I realize that there is something in my whole
manner that dismisses her and it is that something that I am
using to control the conversation and her. There is a way in
which I am paying no attention to her.

The controlling mechanism is almost always unconscious
and automatic. The trick is to hide it from both of us —
which is something I'm pretty good at — to appear available
without being available, to appear to be there but to be some-

place else or no place. Then if she accuses me of ignoring her
— says I'm aloof, distant, and unavailable — I can say she's
crazy — with a good deal of self-righteous anger to back it up.
I can insist she is paranoid.

I am not saying this is the only way I have of relating to
women — although it is a long-standing, regular theme. Over
time, I have more real relationships with more women. I meet
women who refuse to be ignored, who insist on talking about
what is going on with them and between us. It is not that
I am more available than I used to be (although that too) but
that I am not allowed to pretend that I'm there when I'm not
— as much. When I'm afraid of making contact, I have to
say so.

That is why the very literal, specific, concrete, personally
and intuitively authenticated talk that goes on in the Women's
Liberation movement about experience in kitchens and with
families and in seeking recognition in a male world and between men and women seems like such a political breakthrough
to me. It is that very concrete talk that makes me see a world
and people I have known about but ignored. The more general talk about capitalism and the oppression of women, for
example, does not challenge me. That talk can go on for
hours and years without ever coming to grips with what is
actually going on, without forcing people to see how the system of oppression keeps working.

There is also the question of how it all happened — how I
got this ability to ignore women. Partly it is just a basic assumption — a universal assumption — about what women are
that is so conclusive that there is no reason to question it. However, there was a training process about how to enforce the system. I can remember in grade school the satisfaction with which
girls were tormented by and excluded from boys' games. It
felt exclusive and good to know that they wanted to play but
couldn't be let in because they weren't "good enough." The
teasing of girls too — the pranks, breaking up their games (I

can remember running through and stealing hopscotch markers), taunting them about our games — was a way of keeping them interested in our exclusive society. If they had no interest, we wouldn't have felt so important. We needed them to feel bad about being left out. So little girls had to be actively ignored. Their interest had to be solicited in order to be turned aside. In this sense, grade school was relatively out front.

The process of becoming more adult and sophisticated took care of that. As I got older and the masculine stakes got higher, soliciting attention had to be more and more covert in order to deflect the ego blow that would come if my overture was ignored or turned aside. Putting women down as a way to keep them in line and assure their attention became the logical conclusion of the process. It is a direct descendant of stealing hopscotch markers — and it can still be done by "teasing," although it can most easily be done by learning to assume the manner of superiority — the manner of the put-down.

There is a way of course in which I (men) are vulnerable. There is a period of time when the armor of intellectual, physical and moral superiority is being hammered together when boys/men have yet to develop proficiency in maintaining the superior stance. It is this lack of ability that creates the vulnerability or low confidence that leads men to feel "hurt" and "fucked over" by women. It is my inability to sucessfully suppress women, my failure to get a hammer lock on them, that is called hurt. It is a funny kind of hurt, but it does hurt. It pushes me in two directions. The most obvious is toward more effective control — mastery of the discipline of manhood — the subjugation of womanhood. But the hurt also pushes me toward the search for a different kind of relationship with women altogether — a relationship not based on dominance.

In the meantime, there is still a lot of reflex and old fear working to keep women away. There is a line that I do not want women to cross (a tone of voice I do not want them to take with me) and even "smart, competitive women" who know they are as competent as men, are usually smart enough to stay on the right side of it. Crossing the line is very hard — for everybody. So obviously it is easier if the whole issue of who's on top never gets called into question in the first place. It is most "painless" for everyone if it can just be understood that I am superior. And all of this can be quite easily communicated "unconsciously" by tone of voice, authority, ease of speech, just the right amount of involvement, edge, eye contact, hand gestures.

7

I wrote a letter to my mother yesterday in which I tried to break my since-early-childhood pattern of presenting a well-ordered image of myself to her and everybody, but in some ways especially to her. It is the image of me as competent, self-sufficient, clear, thoughtful, under control, blah, bligah. The attempt gave me a headache it was so hard, and was pretty much of a failure to boot. Toward the end, the letter got sort of incoherent and dribbled off into my own spaciness which I guess was somewhat more honest than usual. But the headache hung on, making me think that some part of me really wanted to retract the letter — although I wouldn't, largely because it took too much energy to write it and I really can't contemplate doing it over. Some part of me resists getting a "fresh start" with her, even though I did wake up this morning feeling fresh and wanting to try.

I am really tired of saying one part of me wants this and another part of me wants that. One part of me wants to dance; another part of me is afraid to. One part of me wants to have an affair; another part of me is frightened of the consequences. One part of me wants to shit; another part wants to get off the pot. Bligah, bligah, blah. One part of me can go fuck itself. I don't much care which. Or how about, "One part of me wishes that one part of me would go fuck itself."

I can't say where I'm going. I have precious little to say

about where I'm at that doesn't sound like blah or bligah. (I'm not even sure how to spell bligah. Bliggah?)

It felt good to get up early this morning. Fresh start. I had a long involved dream about Kathy. It was so good to see her and know she was okay — but we couldn't talk. We were in New York and she was hiding and I was paranoid and the weight of the oppression in her little one-room apartment (where she has always lived) made it impossible to talk. She seemed sort of starchy and wasted from hiding and staying in her room too much, a little overweight too. But the contact we had in the dream was real. Maybe the most real we've ever had. I really did feel a lot more about *her* than perhaps I ever have before. When I left she gave me her old, fur-lined army fatigue jacket which I hid in my old, imitation leather briefcase so the cops wouldn't see it. I really do love her a lot.

Since I wrote it two minutes ago, half a dozen ways have occurred to me to diminish the last sentence. They are like announcements that I am back in the real world where I never loved Kathy that much. In the two minutes I also thought about Ezmerelda — the raccoon that lived in the attic above my room the winter in New Hampshire and would occasionally come down the attic stairs to get the food and water I put out for her/him (I have tried to deal with the possibility Ezmerelda is a he). I loved Ezmerelda a lot too — even when she was right there, but then Ezmerelda was an animal. But then so is Kathy. A bear, I think. Or maybe it is less objectifying to say she is a Kathy animal. I like that better. I am a Paul animal. Grrr.

8

I have energy — a great deal. Much of it bottled up — but much of it chafing. It is the energy to get into today's constraint, today's straitjacket and struggle for air within it. It is the energy that returns me to this book to work again for a place to hang in the netting I have constructed. It is the energy to unalienate my work, to bring it home, to make my home my work, to make my work me, to make me, me. Me.

But it is harder to find an adequate release through writing and at times that has made this Postscript seem like a chore. There is another pull. It feels like a deeper pull than the one to write this book. It feels more like me pulling. It feels very much like a pull down and in and away. Away from anonymous you's. Away from amorphous we's. Down and in to me.

The chafing energy wants to be free to live in this place I am in and relate to the people in it. There is so much to do here — so many sensible, practical, personal, communal, political things to be done. And if writing is one of them, I have not particularly felt it. So I feel pulled away to write — pulled away from cooking, from working on the house, from spending time with the people here in doing those things or other things. I feel pushed to get into my head, and although I have tried to get my head into my life in writing this, it is not really the easiest way. There are too many of the old intellectual pitfalls. And I really do want to take the easiest way — because I know that even that is incredibly hard.

When the book is done I am getting a job. As little job as possible. As much time here as possible. After that, there is the rest of my life — and today. Today still has a lot of promise.

Another thing. I really want to be where I am. It feels like the right place to be — which perhaps means a place as good as any other or even a little better. I feel the same about the people who live here. There is nothing very special about us as a group. We simply happened upon one another. But it seems to me that we are as good a group as any to deal with what it would mean to live together as a supporting family — or even a little better. It is a release to me to feel that this is not *the* mystical combination of people who are so far into each other's heads and bodies that they can transcend their limits. I know in the past I have hoped for some such combination to emerge. But that hope really turns into a justification for not dealing with the people around me. There is no way it can all be good vibes.

I am here, in what appears to me to be a very ordinary situation with as much time as I have and a lot of energy. I genuinely dig the ordinariness; I like having energy. I am glad to be here.

9

Nothing ever changes. I am exactly the same now as I have always been. I have always been the same. I will always be the same. Nothing ever changes. I know this is a very airy way to talk, but it is literally what I mean.

I want to give an example. Ann and Leni and I were feeling tense last night. It's not particularly important to say what we were tense about — just that we were tense — the universal tension — tense with ourselves, tight — tense with the world, afraid. We were trying to talk out our tension but it wasn't working. The talk, regardless of the words, kept carrying the tension tone along, the sound of our voices kept drowning out the words. I suggested that we stop talking and try listening to music and maybe dance in order to work out the tension, to listen to other sounds than our own, maybe even move to them. But the suggestion about dancing was mostly to Leni because dancing is still very dangerous for me, and I usually can only do it when I am alone and even then, it is only with real effort (at first) that I can rid myself of the fear of dancing and feeling awkward, my fear of being found clumsy and embarrassing to be around. (This is hard to write.) And I knew that Ann had much of the same trouble I did, but Leni can let go in the presence of other people sometimes and really dance, so it seemed to me that what I was suggesting was that we could all listen to music and maybe Leni would feel loose enough to dance, although in the back of my mind, when I think about it, I realize there may have been some more than ordinary desire in me last night to dance too. I don't recall ever before suggesting to Leni that she might want to dance.

At any rate, after a flurry of disconnections we all wound up in the raccoon room where the record player is, and after some already-in-anticipation-of-music-more-relaxed talk, we turned on a record and Leni began to dance. But what I hadn't counted on happened. Ann got up and started to dance too. And then I got hit hard. I got a full double-barreled blast of sixteen-year-old anguish about my inability to dance. Through some streak of fear and arrogance it had not occurred to me to think that Ann might be able to take a step we both wanted to take before I took it. That has a lot to do with the dynamics of my relationship with Ann. But it also has to do with the dynamics of my relationship with women in general and with people in general, especially when it comes to dancing. My conviction of my own inadequacy as a dancer (a dancing person) is so deep that I find it necessary, in order to salvage some crumb of self-respect, to see it in everybody else. I see the inadequacy and pretense of their movements; I see through their veils to their panic; I become a perfectionist and purist about dancing — a thing which I cannot do. My X-ray vision covers over my envy of anybody who can dance. It also makes people uncomfortable about dancing in my presence — if I can get them to notice me watching them without it showing that I'm watching — if I can project it as an aura. It is still hard for Leni to dance in my presence, even though we have looked at all this together and brushed away some of the secrecy and stale air surrounding these feelings in me. She is freer to take leave of my constraint and understands, I think, that her exercise of the freedom frees me from some of the guilt and tension for having collaborated in the suppression of others (especially loved ones) as well as my own. Still, it is hard for her. And still it is hard for me to let her be with her dancing what she is with her dancing. It is hard not to feel active inferiority with anybody who can dance.

So you can see that Ann's dancing could throw me. Suddenly I was the worst dancer in the place again. The only one who was afraid. At a moment when I was summoning my resolve to set aside some of my paralysis, at a moment, therefore, when I was especially aware of all the old ways of maintaining paralysis, at a moment when I was "vulnerable," I bump, and I fell all the way down, all the way back to sixteen, all the way back to fifteen, all the way back to the first dance I went to in the eighth grade, and I really went all the way back and felt everything again, all the things I have always felt about dancing.

I couldn't move. I couldn't look at Ann — my eyes were instantly ready to see every tension and awkwardness in her body, and yet I felt pure envy and humiliated anger. Leni must have seen my face freeze or maybe she even saw the hurt go down before I could put my face together and fix my eyes on the wall. She stopped dancing and came over and asked what was wrong. I said, "Nothing," just like I'd always said when someone indicated they were aware of my discomfort. But she knew better and kept looking at me and maybe even said (I'm not sure), "Are you sure?" I hesitated and then said, "Something — nothing," but "something" was said inaudibly and immediately punctuated with "nothing." Then I made a look with my eyes that tried to say I couldn't talk, and I think she saw that too, so she stopped looking and just sat beside me while Ann danced through the rest of the song and I looked at the wall. I was literally doubled up during part of the time. Unable to sit up straight, unable to straighten my head or my eyes.

By the time the song was over and another record was put on, I'd gotten a little more control and maybe because Leni knew so much about what was going on with me or maybe because she knew so little (it doesn't much matter), she left the environment of my constraint and went ahead and danced — and got into it — and established her own mood and her own integrity with the music. And I can't tell you what a relief it was when Leni began to dance to feel that I had been seen but not smothered by the reflection, loved in my weakness without allowing my weakness to take over and bring everything to a halt with all eyes focused on it and all activity dominated by it. As she danced, I slowly got my arms around a sixteen-year-old boy dying at a high school Friday night record hop after the football game and held onto him — tight and lovingly — until he felt better — until, in fact, he finally got up and danced in my thirty-one/sixteen-year-old body.

But the dancing was not that important. The fact that I danced in the presence of others (not with — not yet, maybe never — but in the presence of) does not feel all that significant — even though there have been many months and before that over two years and before that years and years when I have wanted to get up and dance but was unable, and before that years when I was unable to admit, even to myself, that I even wanted to dance, and before that years when I tried to dance and hated every excruciating moment of it. So you see it should seem very important. But it doesn't.

The reason it doesn't is because the experience that stands out is still the pain, dying, pit, shame, cringing. The loving for the sixteen-year-old boy is still too hard (not new — it has been there all along — but very difficult) and the anger on his behalf is just beginning to emerge from complete oblivion.

The love can be experienced more deeply but it can never, no matter how strong, no matter how augered it is by anger, erase the pain. To be any good, it must be a love for me in my humiliation. It must be both at once, because both are me. It makes no difference who put the hatred of me in me — I have felt it. I cannot de-experience anything, I cannot purge my life of any of its reality without joining the forces that would make my life unreal. But it does make sense to think of re-experiencing — of experiencing again — perhaps "more deeply." Sometimes I feel that way. I feel like everything is being endlessly

repeated in me. I see myself running through the same set of
problems over and over again, changing the metaphors I use to
think about them with, but always the same set of problems,
throughout my whole life. And usually this makes me feel
weighted down and old. Although if you think about it there
is no logical reason why it shouldn't make me feel young or
ageless since what is happening is everything — my whole life
— happening over again. Everything. All of it. Even the things
I "missed" the first time but now *know* were there. My anger
becomes most intense only when I realize it stretches back
through my whole life — not "realize" it on this piece of
paper, but actually stop and feel it.

Nothing ever changes. But what about re-experiencing more
deeply? Isn't that change? Isn't deepening changing? No it is
not. I do not believe that you can feel anything deeply if you
did not feel it deeply all along. You can imagine something you
felt you felt deeply. To re-experience something is to experience it again — to feel it now as you actually felt it then. And
if I *know* that I felt something, I do not call that imagination.
I call it experience. Imagination is feelings that are not fully
trusted. Imagination is feelings that are not known to be true
feelings because they are not felt strongly enough. To re-
experience something more deeply means in fact to experience
fully what you always felt. Fully. Always.

The meaning of all this is more than I can comprehend. That
is why my writing tends to drift off into being airy. I know
that the words have meaning, but I do not experience it. My
knowledge feels like imagination — knowledge not trusted or
experienced — alienated knowledge. Whereas I do trust completely the knowledge of my anger as a sixteen-year-old or as
a little child. I remember it. I feel it. That means that my own
distinction between imagination and experience is a very critical
one for me. It is the line that I use to discern "where I'm at."
It is the point beyond which I no longer experience reality,

even though I "know" it is *there*. It is the difference between *here* and *there*.

Listen to a letter a friend of ours, Sue Carroll, wrote to us. (Destroying the universe means destroying the wall between experience and imagination, means totally obliterating the distinction.)

Dear All of You.

Sitting on the front porch of my cave refreshing myself with a brief moon bath. The moon is full and lemon yellow. It's almost bright as daylight with the help of a small candle. Had a strange but safe hitch out here. Rode most of the way with two Tennessee hillbillies, Clell and Roland. Have moved myself into Eagle Nest Castle, a fine little cave perched high up on a hill with a commanding view, alas, of the gypsum mine. It's closer to the road and further from the bombing range than Varga Cave. Not the awesome scenery of the Sierras, but I find the desert more conducive to good zazen. A drunken mosquito staggered into my cave tonight, tried to sting me, fell over and died. I'm still puzzling over it. Not as much weeping and gnashing of teeth this time. My faith and resolve are deepening. A daughter of the Dharma, I formed myself in my mother's womb. A baby, I slept in my crib. A child, I watched and wondered at the door. A child, I was taught to read, to speak, to think; was taught to know the important difference between right and wrong, up and down, good and bad, yellow and blue. . . . A young woman I went forth, alone and afraid, into a world I never made. Now, a woman, I sit alone in a cave with my fearless body pitted against the whole universe. I will destroy this universe, this self that you — you my parents, my friends, my enemies — have given me. I will start over at the beginning. I will find out for myself whether a mountain is really a mountain, whether water is really water. What is this life I'm leading; is it real; is it real? I will find an answer to all those childish questions that were laughingly brushed aside. Why isn't everything nothing? Well, who made God then? Why do people fight? How do I know this isn't just a dream? I will find my True Self. Ha! The full moon has a way of kindling my inner fires, so I'll go back inside and take advantage of it. Will mail this when I go out for supplies. Be kind to your-selves.

Love,
Susan

P.S. Did the garden get thinned? The lettuce will need room to head up. The peas can probably stay as they are. Did the potatoes ever come up? And the roof?

I have just begun to explore what lies buried in my imagina-tion, untrusted and unexplored. Sue has gone further. In her voice, the incongruity of a drunk mosquito — dying — a gyp-sum mine — a bombing range and a baby consciously forming itself in its mother's womb, begin to dissolve. It says, "What is so incongruous? These are the things that are happening. I know. I have experienced all of them." But I have not. Al-though I tend to believe it is true. Blah, bligah.

So where does it all end? Where does blah meet bligah and become God? What will you think of me now that I've added all this? Will you think me more vain or less? Will I care? Where do I end? Where do I end and Sue take up? Where does Sue end? Where does this book end?

And although I'm not particularly interested in most of those questions, I will take up the one of where the book ends. Because it seems to me that it can end right about here. This book has come about as far as it can go — as far as I can make it go — as far as I want it to go.

I am reasonably satisfied with where it ends — although a blah in me — as always — feels I owe you an apology for not having a better wrap-up. But then as I think about it, the issue of your satisfaction or mine does not seem very important. Satisfaction "with something" is such a nebulous, summary feeling.

Trust your experience.

Trust your imagination.

Do whatever is necessary to create that trust.

There is no other place to be than the one you are in now. There is no place to go. There is nothing to get ready for.

Where are you now? Who are you with? What are you doing? What is actually happening?

Did the garden get thinned?

The lettuce will need room to head up. The peas can probably stay as they are.

Did the potatoes ever come up?

And the roof?

10

The most pressing problem of the moment seems quite literally to figure out how to stay alive — which has necessitated more thinking about dying and madness than I have ever done before. I am in trouble. We are in trouble. There is enormous tension. There are enormous fights. There is awful depression. There is Leni thinking actively about suicide. There is me toying with suicide fantasies for the first time ever. There are six other people (including one two-year-old) who are very fucked up (even though Pat and Ken seem to me to be very in touch with themselves in many ways — in touch enough to be willing to really look hard at how fucked up they are) and one relatively, remarkably unfucked up one-and-a-half-year-old who is still, most of the time, a creature of a very different, incredibly more intuitive world

than the one we live in. There is more love than I ever believed possible. There is frequently the feeling that we are
spiraling forever downward into ourselves.

The revolutionary struggle, as I see it, is to figure out a way
to stay alive and be alive. I have my whole life in front of me,
literally falling away in front of me like some great chasm
opening up from where I sit, and I know no *way* through it.
I do not know *what* will keep me going. There is no what.
There is only me and my life. The anonymous "out there in
the world" that I grew up to be something in is dissolving.
Leni also wanted to be something — even more than I did
(do), largely I think because for women it is made so hu-
miliatingly unattainable to be "anything."

The tension is mine. There is no use combating or suppress-
ing it. When it is here it can either be resisted or experienced.
When it is experienced, there is a sense in which it is useful.
It may be unpleasant or worse, but it is useful.

Today is a more together day — so far. Last night was a
stupor. Really flattened — foggy — afraid but also beyond fear
in some way — half from being numb, half from feeling that
whatever is next that we're struggling to fend off can't be that
much more oppressive and frightening than where we're at
now.